THE
ITALIAN RENAISSANCE
IN ITS
HISTORICAL BACKGROUND

BY

DENYS HAY

Professor of Medieval History
University of Edinburgh

CAMBRIDGE
AT THE UNIVERSITY PRESS
1961

0/9263.

RS
156816
945.05 HAY

Published by the Syndics of the Cambridge University Press
Bentley House, 200 Euston Road, London NW1 2DB
American Branch: 32 East 57th Street, New York, N.Y.10022

© Cambridge University Press 1961

ISBNs

0 521 05234 3 hard covers
0 521 09398 8 paperback

First published 1961
Reprinted with minor corrections 1962
Reprinted 1966
First paperback edition 1966
Reprinted 1970, 1973

First printed in Great Britain at the University Press, Cambridge
Reprinted in Great Britain by
Hazell Watson & Viney Ltd,
Aylesbury, Bucks

945.05

THE
ITALIAN RENAISSANCE
IN ITS
HISTORICAL BACKGROUND

THE WILES LECTURES
GIVEN AT THE QUEEN'S UNIVERSITY
BELFAST 1960

CONTENTS

STORIA POLITICA D' ITALIA
SCRITTA DA UNA SOCIETÀ D'AMICI

SOTTO LA DIREZIONE

DI

PASQUALE VILLARI

STORIA

DELLE

SIGNORIE ITALIANE

DAL 1313 AL 1530

NARRATA DA

CARLO CIPOLLA

VOLUME QUARTO

Parte II.ª

ANTICA CASA EDITRICE
DOTT. FRANCESCO VALLARDI
MILANO

BOLOGNA   FIRENZE   NAPOLI   ROMA   TORINO
Farini, 10   Alfani, 41.   Monteoliveto, 70.   Convertite, 8.   Carlo Alberto, 8.

THE COVER OF THE 1881 EDITION OF CIPOLLA'S
'STORIA DELLE SIGNORIE ITALIANE'

LIST OF ILLUSTRATIONS

PLATES

List of Illustrations

Acknowledgments are due to the London Library for the Cipolla; to the Albertina, Vienna, for Plate II; to Giraudon for Plates I and IV; to the Italian State Tourist Office, London, for Plates V and IX; to J. Allan Cash for Plate XVII; to the Trustees of the British Museum for Plate XXIV; to Mansell for Plate XVIII; to Mansell–Anderson for Plates VI, XI, XVI, XIX, XXII and XXIII; and to Mansell–Alinari for Plates VII, VIII, X, XII, XIII, XIV and XV.

MAP

PREFACE

ACKNOWLEDGMENTS usually come at the end of a preface. This must begin with several.

In 1957 the Syndics of the Cambridge University Press invited me to write a volume on the Italian Renaissance and I accepted their invitation. When I was asked a year later to deliver the Wiles Lectures in The Queen's University of Belfast it seemed to me that the subject I had promised to write about would be suitable for the lectures. The Syndics agreed to this suggestion and I am grateful to them for their approval of my change of plan.

The remarkable foundation established by Mrs Janet P. Boyd in memory of her father provides not only a lecturer but also part of his audience. To the discussions which followed each lecture I am indebted for a few corrections and much valuable comment; I should add that in the discussion the visitors were joined by some very lively Belfast historians; to both groups I wish to express my thanks. To Professor Michael Roberts, Mrs Janet P. Boyd, and the Vice-Chancellor and Mrs Grant I am obliged for much personal kindness. It is a pleasure to pay tribute to the resources of the Warburg Institute Library and to the unfailing courtesy of Mr J. B. Trapp.

The four lectures as written proved to be considerably too long for delivery and were abbreviated as spoken. For the printed version I have divided them into chapters and extended them further, mainly by inserting a section (chapter II) on the notion of the Renaissance as an epoch, since it was plain from our discussions that, however self-evident the concept may be to those of us who work in this field, it is less so for historians who are concerned with other ages.

I have tried to keep annotation to a minimum and I am well aware how greatly I have benefited from books and articles not here mentioned and from scholars here and in Italy with whom I have talked. (At the suggestion of the Press a list of works referred to in notes has been added, in which the works of greatest significance have been marked with an asterisk in the hope that this will be of service to those readers who wish to take the subject farther on their own.) To mention everything relevant would have produced a work which would have been excessively armoured for its task. This task is to provoke an unbiased and fresh appraisal of a phase in Italian and European history which has, more than most such 'periods', suffered from traditional and stereotyped treatment, above all by being dealt with as static and solid. We must have epochs and I have tried to say later in this book why the Renaissance seems to me to have characteristics which make it convenient to treat it as a unit. But within our arbitrary units we must accommodate change and see that general concepts are our servants, not our masters. In this sense all 'periods' are 'transitional periods', the Renaissance like the rest.

In all that follows I am at many points implicitly, and sometimes explicitly, at variance with the judgments and the approach of Jacob Burckhardt in his *Civilization of*

Preface

the Renaissance in Italy, first published at Basle exactly a century ago (August 1860). Yet like all who have become prisoners of Renaissance Italy I was captured by Burckhardt. I first read his book in 1932 and I can still remember the excitement that it produced in me: it was history with a new dimension, for this attitude to the past, this attempt at a total view, had not yet been practised in other periods or really very much by other historians. Since then I have read the book through twice, once in a spirit of sharp criticism, and a third time with a growing admiration of his mastery in handling so subtly and so humbly the most difficult of all material. John of Salisbury (who joined our debates at Belfast once or twice) compared moderns to dwarfs astraddle the shoulders of the ancients. If we can see farther or better nowadays than Buckhardt we owe it largely to his example that we see in this way at all. One other author, nearly contemporary with Burckhardt, I should like to mention: John Addington Symonds. His *Renaissance in Italy* (1875–86) is a remarkable and neglected work; again and again it anticipates some of the judgments of recent scholars and it is unjust to dismiss it as a kind of prolix English version of Burckhardt.

Now that we are detached from the Renaissance, as nineteenth-century scholars were not, we can, I believe, begin to judge it more surely. Yet much remains to be done—in political, economic, artistic and literary history—before we can talk with confidence about it. If the tasks are not daunting it is because the Renaissance is the last epoch when one man can hope to have a direct view of most of the sources. He may not be able to master more than a small section of them, but like the medievalist and unlike the modernist, he can feel the whole texture and attempt a general view of the whole of a substantial period of time, as I here try to view the history of Italy from the early fourteenth century to the mid-sixteenth.

D.H.

EDINBURGH
July 1960

My thanks are now due to Mr Giles Robertson for reading the typescript before it went to the Press, and to Dr Nicolai Rubinstein and Professor Roberto Weiss for reading the proofs.

It has not been possible to revise this book for the present reprint, but a few verbal alterations have been introduced.

May 1966

D.H.

CHAPTER I

INTRODUCTION

THE subject of the lectures here rearranged and printed is one which has for long been argued over by historians. By way of introduction certain assumptions should be stated. In this way my attitude towards some of the controversies will be clear from the start and a few terms, often used in differing senses by different writers, will be defined.

To start with, I accept as a fact that there was a Renaissance in the period (to beg a few questions at any rate for the time being) between about 1350 and about 1700. I accept that this Renaissance occurred first in Italy in the fourteenth and fifteenth centuries and that it later affected to a greater or lesser degree the rest of Europe. I say this with confidence because to my mind the evidence is overwhelming. Look at the façade of S. Maria Novella at Florence where the early fourteenth-century base rises to flower in Alberti's mid-fifteenth-century design; walk into the Cathedral at Chartres, through the tremendous chords of Gothic harmony, and pause before the new delicacy of the screen round the choir where from the early sixteenth century the story of Mary is illustrated in a quite different manner [Plates I, IV]. Think for a moment of old St Peter's and new St Peter's in Rome [Plates II, III]; of old St Paul's and new St Paul's in London. Think of Dante, Chaucer and Villon on the one hand and of Ariosto, Ronsard and Milton on the other. Think of

Aquinas *de regimine principum* and then of Machiavelli and Castiglione.

I am far from trying to say that in the course of the Renaissance everything changed. The past is not a Christmas pantomime and seldom if ever deals in transformation scenes. Older attitudes and techniques persist unadulterated or only thinly diluted with the new. Aristotle and Aquinas have a fresh lease of life in the sixteenth century, in Italy as in the North. The subjects of Ariosto and Spenser are medieval and so too perhaps is part of their irony. Yet when these and a thousand similar points are allowed for there is still a difference in the style of living between the Renaissance and both what came before and what came after.

The phrase 'style of living' has been chosen with some care, for it conveys, or is meant to convey, the whole outward character of life.[1] That is to say, to the criticism that the Renaissance made little or no difference to the domestic behaviour of men and women—to Mr Eliot's 'birth, copulation and death'—I have no answer save to say that this is not history. To the criticism that politicians are thugs and that Henry VIII or Francis I or Charles V could learn nothing of the art of government from the Medici or the Borgia or Machiavelli, to the criticism, that is to say, that the facts of political life remained unchanged by the Renaissance, I would reply that this is only partly true: for the princes of the Renaissance period found new strength,

---

[1] That is, something rather wider than applying the artistic concept of 'style' to 'other fields of intellectual history', as suggested by P. O. Kristeller in his essay 'Humanism and Scholasticism in the Italian Renaissance', *Studies in Renaissance Thought and Letters* (Rome 1956), p. 554, a study which in many ways is the most significant general survey of the whole problem which has appeared in recent years; I am greatly indebted to it.

Introduction

both administrative and theoretical, in this period and because of the developments we shall shortly consider. To the criticism that the Renaissance left untouched the basic economy of Europe I will not return the dusty answer that someone or other has to dig the potatoes; for it seems to me significant that the changes we are to consider did in fact impose new demands on the productive forces of Europe—mainly agrarian—and that the wealth of the land was routed towards the satisfaction of new needs. We are, I would concede, not faced with significant technological changes in this period; it is, indeed, one of those paradoxical epochs when cultural change seems to be out of step with economic change.[1] Nor was the discovery of the New World of much economic significance: Alexander VI had the ceiling of S. Maria Maggiore in Rome gilded with the first American gold.

This last gesture hints at what I am trying to say. The style of living is what in a sense changes in history and history is about what changes. And the style of living does not only involve clothes and buildings and decoration; it involves the justification of the kind of life we lead, the adjustment between duty and pleasure, the way we learn and what we learn, the way we pray and what we pray for. In this vast domain, the territory of our public purposes, the period of the Renaissance witnesses enormous innovations which I shall try to describe in these pages.

[1] This question has been discussed by R. S. Lopez, 'Still another Renaissance', *Amer. Hist. Rev.* LVII (1951–2), 1–21; A. Sapori, 'Medio evo e rinascimento, spunti per una diversa periodizzazione', *Archivio storico italiano*, CXV (1957), 135–64; Delio Cantimori, 'Il problema rinascimentale proposto da Armando Sapori', reprinted in *studi di storia* (Florence 1959), pp. 366–78. For a brief note on the economic regression of the fourteenth and fifteenth centuries see below, p. 67.

3

One further objection may be lodged at this point: that the changes to which I refer affect only a tiny proportion of the population, leaving untouched the masses, for whom the moral innovations and new developments in literature and art to which I have just referred were remote, the concern of their 'betters'. I am convinced that this denial of the validity of the importance of ideas is misconceived. There is, of course, a history (largely unwritten as yet) of the notions common to the uneducated, or the non-educated: the assumptions and attitudes of the man in the street or the man behind the plough. It records a current which moves very deeply, so deeply perhaps that it will never be possible to dredge up the submerged monuments which sometimes deflect its slow course. But, in so far as one can discern these, they were fashioned in the castle rather than in the cottage and are absorbed by the illiterate and the unsophisticated as symbols or superstitions, in that curious combination of earthy common sense and pro-pitiatory religion which make up the lives of those innocent of higher abstractions and ambitions. It took centuries for the mythology of the Christian religion and some of its moral attitudes as seen by the Fathers to penetrate the common consciousness of the West; it takes centuries before some of the ideas discussed in this book (including a new version of what constituted Christian duty) reach down to simple men and women. To that extent intellec-tual history—in common with political history and much economic and social history—deals with an *élite*, and this is perhaps still true of our own day. Admittedly one is tempted in this field to anticipate the long-term diffusion, the vulgarization, of arts and ideas—to talk about Abelard or Aquinas, Petrarch or Bruni, Copernicus or Descartes as if their influence was immediately widespread. One must guard against this temptation and, as far as the following pages are concerned, I claim only that the notions we are to consider went far to colouring the attitudes of the *haute bourgeoisie*, the gentry and nobility and the princes, first of all in Italy and then in Europe generally, during the centuries I dub 'Renaissance'. These groups were, however, those which were politically and socially dominant.

I do not think that a general discussion of the Italian Renaissance is uncalled for, however inadequate my own qualifications to undertake the task. In the last thirty or so years there has been a very large number of specialist studies of aspects of the Renaissance in Italy and a few (all too few) of the Renaissance in Europe as a whole. Yet I cannot think of any place where the questions are treated in a general way, where the whole subject is reviewed. There are of course good reasons for this. The most obvious one is the huge bulk of the detailed critical work now available in books and periodical literature. The very thought of this has a paralysing effect. Consider for example the very large but very selective bibliography published by Federico Chabod;[1] count the number of journals in Europe and North America devoted more or less exclusively to the Renaissance; remember that nearly all historical periodicals publish Renaissance work from time to time. How can one man survey all this? I hasten to confess that I have not and that I am sometimes filled with gloomy apprehension at the thought of it.

[1] *Machiavelli and the Renaissance* (London 1958), pp. 201–47.

Undoubtedly this has led to the subject as a whole being regarded as, in a practical way, unmanageable and explains why there has been a tendency to discuss the Renaissance on the level of historiography, as in the indispensable work of Wallace K. Ferguson,[1] or on the level of methodology as in the essays (to quote only the names of two scholars) of E. F. Jacob[2] and Delio Cantimori,[3] where the notion of the Renaissance as a period is debated. That is not to say that there have not been some very useful studies of the Renaissance in the framework of general histories of Europe: M. P. Gilmore's volume comes to mind[4] and (though less happy) A. Renaudet's contribution to the relevant volumes of the series 'Peuples et Civilisations';[5] but it is to say that, despite their very great value, the essays by Garin and Toffanin and Kristeller remain partial studies of what we are concerned with here: indeed their authors would not claim more for them than that.[6]

A survey of Renaissance history is thus in a sense a desideratum of our day and in trying to provide it I can claim only that I have tried to read some of the most important secondary works and as much of the original literature as possible.

The need for a survey of Renaissance Italy is, I believe, even more necessary for another reason. From Voigt

[1] *The Renaissance in Historical Thought*, Cambridge, Mass. 1948.

[2] '"Middle Ages" and "Renaissance"', *Essays in the Conciliar Epoch*, Manchester 1953, pp. 170–84.

[3] 'La periodizzazione dell'età del Rinascimento', *Studi di storia*, pp. 340–65. This originally appeared in the *Relazioni* of the X Congress of Historical Sciences, Rome 1955.

[4] *The World of Humanism, 1453–1517*, New York 1952.

[5] *La Fin du moyen âge*, 2 vols., Paris 1931; *Les Débuts de l'âge moderne*, Paris 1929.

[6] See references below, pp. 207–12.

and Burckhardt onwards there has been a tendency to divorce the political, social and economic development of Italy from its cultural development. Burckhardt certainly devoted the first part of his book to the history of the peninsula, but then went on in the rest of the work to deal quite independently with the 'Civilization' of his title. Others have taken this kind of approach much farther. On the whole the general historians of Italy for the last half-century, the authors of the standard manuals,[1] completely ignore the Renaissance, while the historians of culture almost completely ignore political and economic history. There has in the last ten years been a remarkable change in this respect: the name of Hans Baron[2] will come to the minds of some readers, and the manual by Nino Valeri.[3] These lectures are offered as a further modest contribution to the furtherance of the same trend.

To embark, however modestly, on the study of Italian history has its own hazards. If one is appalled by the bulk of writing on the cultural side of the Renaissance, what must one feel in front of the erudition displayed by Italian and other scholars towards the political development of Italy? Italy must surely have more learned historical journals of importance than any other country of its size. These contain articles which from time to time make all general surveys partial and out of date. On top of that we must add the series of record publications. And on top of that there is the incredibly rich untapped archive material of many Italian towns, where an active researcher is often ready to contradict and confuse the visiting historian in search of manageable generalizations. Here

[1] See below, p. 43. [2] See below, p. 112. [3] See below, p. 44.

again only someone foolhardy would venture on the task of integrating the cultural history with the political and social history of the peninsula.

This, however, must be attempted. We have for far too long been content in broad discussion of the Renaissance to see it as an unchanging situation, marked by qualities which were treated as if they were commodities in a grocer's shop: from the jar labelled 'humanism' a parcel was made up and sent to Naples or France or Poland; other jars contained 'realism', 'classicism', and (perhaps more reasonably) 'Platonism', 'Neo-Platonism', 'Petrarchism'. Of all these dead 'isms' the most pernicious is the word 'humanism'. On the one hand it has been lifted out of history to become a kind of permanent emotional state, applicable to Abelard or the modern existentialist; on the other hand it has been applied indiscriminately to anyone in the fifteenth or sixteenth centuries who wrote a line or two of Latin or Greek. Kristeller's plea[1] that it should be confined to the grammarian is one which I for one shall try to respond to: I hope in these pages not again to use the word 'human*ism*'.[2] And it will be my aim to deal as far as I am able with the Renaissance as a series of events *in time*, changing with time and place, as a part of history, that is to say. This means that I make no distinction between the Italian Renaissance and the Renaissance in Italy. In pursuing the Renaissance I shall be pursuing the history of Italy itself.

---

[1] P. O. Kristeller, *The Classics and Renaissance Thought*, Cambridge, Mass. 1955, pp. 8–11. On the word 'humanist' see further below, p. 135.

[2] Save for quotations; I should add that this has cost quite an effort and that —in common I imagine with many other teachers—I find the 'ism' too convenient a piece of academic obfuscation to renounce altogether.

I   THE WEST DOOR OF CHARTRES CATHEDRAL

II OLD ST PETER'S, ROME

III NEW ST PETER'S, ROME

These preliminaries have brought us *in medias res.* I must now invite the reader to await further consideration of the points thus far discussed and to view briefly the reasonableness of each of the two terms in the title of this book: 'Renaissance' and 'Italy'. Each might be regarded as self-evident. Each, I believe, is question-begging unless it is clearly defined.

CHAPTER II

THE RENAISSANCE AS A PERIOD IN EUROPEAN HISTORY

As used in the title of these lectures and in the text of the book, the word 'Renaissance' means a period of time and certain characteristics associated with the period. It is on all fours with Middle Ages, Victorian and other similar labels. It is perhaps more liable to beget confusion than these for two reasons. It is a term which was more or less invented at the time and not, as with most such names, a great deal later. And it implies by itself a key idea—that of rebirth—which may lead the unwary into feeling that it has an inevitability denied to other categories; that one can, so to speak, handle its pure gold while 'Middle Ages' and 'Victorian' are mere monies of account. We are, it appears to me, thus faced at the outset with two questions: how does the term Renaissance emerge and how valid a notion is it? are we justified in identifying for separate treatment a period—whether or not called 'Renaissance'—in the centuries lying between the medieval and the modern?

The history of the notion of rebirth is a long one and it has been much written about.[1] From our point of view the significant steps were taken by Italians, and especially Florentines, when reflecting on their own history and especially on their own cultural history. It is in the field

[1] For what follows see in general Wallace K. Ferguson, *The Renaissance in Historical Thought*, chapters 1 and 3 and references.

of Latin letters and the fine arts that, from the fourteenth century onwards, an increasing number of statements are to be found which condemn the trough of time between the end of the ancient world and the Trecento as a period of darkness, where there is no eloquence, no poetry, no great sculpture or painting. We find this attitude in Petrarch and Boccaccio, in Salutati and Bruni, and in the artists and architects of the great age—Ghiberti and Alberti. As an example of this kind of awareness, here are some remarks by the Florentine Matteo Palmieri (1406–75), whose *Vita Civile* will often be quoted in later pages:

Where was the painter's art till Giotto tardily restored it? A caricature of the art of human delineation! Sculpture and architecture, for long years sunk to the merest travesty of art, are only today in process of rescue from obscurity; only now are they being brought to a new pitch of perfection by men of genius and erudition. Of letters and liberal studies at large it were best to be silent altogether. For these, the real guides to distinction in all the arts, the solid foundation of all civilization, have been lost to mankind for 800 years and more. It is but in our own day that men dare boast that they see the dawn of better things. For example, we owe it to our Leonardo Bruni that Latin, so long a bye-word for its uncouthness, has begun to shine forth in its ancient purity, its beauty, its majestic rhythm. Now, indeed, may every thoughtful spirit thank God that it has been permitted to him to be born in this new age, so full of hope and promise, which already rejoices in a greater array of nobly-gifted souls than the world has seen in the thousand years that have preceded it.[1]

This rhapsody, the fervour of which we shall have to account for in later pages, was written in the mid 1430's.

The turn for the better in letters was variously ascribed

[1] *Della vita civile*, ed. F. Battaglia (Scrittori politici Italiani 14), Bologna 1944, pp. 36–7; trans. from W. H. Woodward, *Studies in Education during the Age of the Renaissance*, Cambridge 1906, p. 67.

to Dante, to Petrarch and his contemporaries, or (as in the passage just quoted from Palmieri) to Bruni; in the fine arts Cimabue and Giotto were regarded as pioneers. At the same time the historians, and especially Leonardo Bruni and Flavio Biondo, proceeded as though the break between antiquity and what followed occurred with the barbarian invasions culminating in the sack of Rome in A.D. 410. Biondo in a passage of his *Italia illustrata* discussed later in this book[1] linked together fourteenth-century innovations in letters and politics, making this a fresh general turning-point. In this way the *middle* ages were born. A sense of historical distance was achieved both with regard to the ancient world, for which the artists and writers of fourteenth- and fifteenth-century Italy felt affinity, and with regard to the centuries when, as they felt, art and letters had been neglected. In this way also was born a new sense of style—the *maniera* of the critics from Ghiberti onwards—which enabled the artist to distinguish as never before what was appropriate to given periods of architecture and painting. These processes reach their ultimate point of development in the *Lives* of the artist Giorgio Vasari.[2] From this point onwards Italians and Europeans in general came to accept a Gothic period of the arts associated with a 'medieval' period of history, followed by 'modern' art and history.

The victory in Italy of the new styles, and the occasion for their rapid assimilation outside Italy, are the theme of this study and we may anticipate the outcome by noting

---

[1] Below, pp. 34–8.
[2] *Le vite de' più eccellenti architetti, pittori et scultori italiani da Cimabue insino a tempi nostri*, Florence 1550. See Ferguson, pp. 59–67.

now that one of the most remarkable results has been a general division of European history into medieval and modern. Each country has its own boundary for this, adapted to its own development. For France 'modern' history dates from the invasion of Italy in 1494; for England it starts with the advent of the Tudors in 1485; in Spain it is the union of Castile and Aragon in 1479 and in Germany the election of Charles V as emperor in 1519. In this way the Renaissance has been treated as ushering in the modern world—a doctrine which was elaborated in the second half of the nineteenth century, above all by Jacob Burckhardt in his *Civilization of the Renaissance in Italy* (1860).

Criticisms of these attitudes to the past have been frequent and often acrid. In particular the Renaissance condemnation of medieval barbarism has been challenged during the last hundred years by many historians. It has been shown how original as well as beautiful are the buildings and decorations of Gothic Christendom, how vigorous were its social and political institutions, how strong and noble the researches of its philosophers and scientists. Moreover the very field of literary revival or rebirth has been asserted to belong to the medieval North: we have been reminded that a love of letters, an eager cultivation of the Latin classics, is as characteristic of France and England in the twelfth century, of the court of Charlemagne in the ninth, as of the Italian cities in the time of Petrarch and his successors. With much of this any dispassionate person must agree. It is no longer possible to talk, as humanists did, of medieval darkness and obscurantism. And if one feels that the handful of scholars who constitute the 'Carolingian Renaissance', the coteries—who lacked all public patronage—in Chartres and Paris in the days of John of Salisbury, are somewhat esoteric as they were certainly uninfluential, this is not to refuse to the middle ages its own unique and invaluable contributions to literature and art. One further denunciation—that 'Renaissance' is a misnomer because what was being done in letters and art was original and in no sense a revival of antiquity—is not worth bothering about. Time and again (especially in cultural and religious history) we find new wine being poured from old bottles.

What seems to many nowadays to be indefensible in the older approach is its attempt to make the Renaissance the herald of what we now regard as our world.[1] What has the Renaissance contributed to the railway engine, the aeroplane, mass education and the ideal of popular government? We live in a world where Latin letters are remote from our present anxieties and pleasures, where even our art and architecture have left the norms set up in the sixteenth century. Beyond that we live, for better and for worse, in *one* world: Africa, Asia, the Americas are daily present, politically and economically and culturally, in our Europe; as Europe is present elsewhere: this is all very different from earlier ages when the traditional geographical limits of Europe represented the furthest bounds of most European activity. This modern world emerged out of its predecessor. Are we justified in treating the preceding epoch as a unit, whether or not we accept for it the term Renaissance? To my mind the answer must be

[1] Cf. Mario M. Rossi, 'Note sulla modernità del Rinascimento', *Nuova rivista storica*, XXXIV (1950).

yes, and the justification for accepting as useful a period embracing what we clumsily call at present 'late-medieval, early modern' can be provided in a brief survey of the main evidence—in politics, economics and in intellectual development.[1]

As far as the political structure of Europe is concerned, it will surely be agreed that the fifteenth and sixteenth centuries were the age of kings. This is obvious enough for the sixteenth century. But the upheavals in France in the early fifteenth century and a little later in England are strong evidence of the power of monarchy, for in both cases the contending magnates sought not to destroy monarchy, but to dominate it for their own purposes. This is clear too from the virtually uninterrupted accretion of power to the English crown from Edward I onwards, so that the machinery taken over by Henry VII was stronger, not weaker, than anything of the kind before, while in France, from Philip IV and Charles V later sovereigns such as Charles VII and Louis XI inherited an administration which again was growing daily in tenacious penetration into all spheres of French public life. Is it not from the later middle ages, so called, that the strong German principates must be dated, the Golden Bull of 1356 offering

[1] The following pages are taken from my paper to the Anglo-American Conference of Historians, London, July 1951; a short summary appeared in the *Bulletin of the Institute of Historical Research*, xxv (1952), 26–7. It points my argument that, although much of what I had to say dealt with the fourteenth and fifteenth centuries, the paper was allocated to the section on 'Modern English History'. I recall applying successively for posts in two Universities in 1938 and being told by each that I could not be considered—in the one case because I was a medievalist, in the other case because I was a modernist: all because I was researching in a late fifteenth-, early sixteenth-century subject—or so I hoped!

a convenient date for the start of the process? Does it not seem improbable that the sixteenth-century monarchy *par excellence*, that of Spain, should have resulted merely from a happy marriage in 1469 rather than from the preceding century of growing bureaucratic centralization in the as yet separate kingdoms? Professor Herbert Butterfield has written: 'It does seem that before the Reformation some wind in the world had clearly set itself to play on the side of kings.'[1] This 'wind in the world' was blowing strongly through the fourteenth, fifteenth, sixteenth and seventeenth centuries, reaching hurricane force at times. From Philip the Fair to Louis XIV, France and the monarchy are interchangeable terms, however one looks at the political history of the period: and more especially in foreign policy is this the case—dynasticism is the only key.

The practice of monarchy in the fourteenth and succeeding centuries had a theory to reinforce it. Notions of sovereignty were in the air at the end of the thirteenth century, as Dr W. Ullmann and others have shown. Paradoxically, it was the Church which hit on the first watertight formula: 'Porro subesse Romano pontifici omni humanae creaturae declaramus, dicimus, et definimus, omnino esse de necessitate salutis.' This categorical statement in *Unam Sanctam* (1302) is more revolutionary than its expropriation, in a secular sense, by Marsilio of Padua twenty years later. Marsilio's *Defensor Pacis* was too academic for the rough and tumble empiricism of fourteenth-century monarchs, though we may note that Henry VIII of England took an interest in a suitably doctored version of a book which seemed to offer a justification

[1] *The Whig Interpretation of History*, London 1931, p. 53.

of the omnipotence of Tudor monarchy. Far more useful to the contemporaries of Marsilio was the virtual stranglehold which kings had over popes: the first of the concordats is really implicit in the Statutes of Provisors and Praemunire (1351, 1353 and subsequent reissues) which finally made the king, not the pope, master of the hierarchy in England. And in the fifteenth century there grew up that doctrine of Divine Right (first in Germany and Spain, be it noted) which was to be a more congenial prop to monarchs than the ambiguous arguments of Aristotelians and Averroists. In defining papal sovereignty the Papacy made, however, only one of its contributions to the strengthening of lay monarchy. The papal court of the thirteenth and fourteenth centuries was an object lesson in administrative efficiency; the bureaucracy of curia and camera, the use of international banking houses, the employment of mercenary armies—these were all devices which kings could borrow from the pope and develop on a vastly grander scale. Even before the end of the thirteenth century St Thomas Aquinas wrote: 'The pope has a plenitude of pontifical power *like a king in a kingdom*'; it was soon to be the case that kings, being their own popes in both Catholic and Reformed communities, could laugh at claims expressed in terms so curiously flattering to themselves. Of course the most impressive evidence for the ubiquity of monarchy lies in the country where the strongest republican and municipal tradition existed—Italy. Here, where oligarchic rule had flourished unchecked, the fourteenth century witnessed the rise of indigenous principates, as we shall see later.

The urban middle class of the fourteenth to seventeenth

centuries was, generally speaking, not averse to strong monarchy. On the contrary, one of the most significant features of the period I am trying to describe is the understanding which existed between town and crown. Tacit, for the most part, even concealed beneath courtly contempt and municipal servility, this alliance was the product of an overwhelming community of political and economic interest. Another group is rising in importance, also (for the most part) in association with the crown: the gentry. All over Europe from the fourteenth century onwards the lesser landholder is becoming more noticeable, more literate, more politically ambitious.

With this all-too-brief picture of 'late medieval' and 'early modern' politics, contrast for a moment what had gone before, what was to come later. Earlier we are in a world of landed magnates, power is decentralized, 'feudalism' totally devoid of a political theory. The king, it is true, survives this twilight of monarchy: he is often himself a great baron; he is hedged by a divinity of sorts. But real power lies with the independent magnates, supreme, when they care, in the king's *entourage*, supreme in that 'manorial system' which fed and clothed themselves and their followers. If we turn to the later period, the world we live in ourselves, we find it dominated by middle-class values in politics, as in economics and art; we live, so to speak, in a parliamentary world; this is true of the monarchies, and it is true of the dictatorships. The theory of republicanism is now universal, socialism and even communism becoming (at any rate in large areas) the refuge of the humdrum and the respectable. The kings have departed in all but name.

In the realm of economic and social structures the evidence for continuity in the period I am discussing seems to me to be overwhelming. The European world of the fourteenth, fifteenth, sixteenth and seventeenth centuries saw an extraordinary balance between cash values and land values. It was a world of banks yet without banknotes; of commerce without industry; of enormous financial operations in an atmosphere almost devoid of financial security; where one had capital, so to speak, without capitalism; where town and country were almost evenly matched in economic importance; where money might be made in a hundred and one ways, but where the only long-term investment was land. Even the revolutionary movements which mark the period are significant: they are almost entirely agrarian, for social liberty had been identified, yet they were nearly all in urbanized areas, for it was in the towns that the identification of social liberty had been realized.

Again, we find a marked contrast between earlier and later periods. In the 'early middle ages' land, as has often been said, was virtually the only source of wealth; there were no peasant risings worth the name before 1200. Money and merchants always existed, it seems, even in the darkest part of the Dark Ages, but they were insignificant. Looking on the other hand at the modern period proper we find that land, though still a source of social prestige, is little else, except when operated industrially. Above all, for over a century the main pace-maker in social and economic affairs has been industry rather than commerce; and the social upheavals in the modern world have arisen from the claims of a proletariat, faintly foreshadowed in fourteenth-century Flanders and Florence, which is fundamentally urban, not agrarian.

Finally we come to the religious, intellectual, literary and artistic features of the 'later medieval–early modern' period. The most obvious characteristic of the intellectual situation (to use an awkward phrase) of these centuries is that it is essentially *lay* and yet essentially *Christian*. The agnostics and atheists are so few that we may forget about them: they are heralds and harbingers, no more. The bulk of the intelligentsia was Christian and yet the impetus to devotion had certainly passed out of the hands of the clergy. The mystical movements of the period are predominantly lay both in composition and leadership, from the Brethren of the Common Life to the Jansenists. What is there *priestly* about Gerard de Groot, Erasmus or Pascal? They reflect, indeed, that preoccupation with the world which is found in the friars: Giuseppe Toffanin has said, with some justice, that the Counter-Reformation begins with St Francis and St Dominic.[1] Certainly no one could accuse the Jesuits (might one not describe them as the most secular of the religious?) in the sixteenth and seventeenth centuries of neglecting this world, in their gallant battle to make the hereafter palatable here below. As a result of the lay direction of Christian spirituality, this epoch is also marked by a series of heresies and schisms: both seem endemic between the fourteenth and the seventeenth centuries, the very instruments designed to meet them, like the friars and the sixteenth-century reformers, leading to further division. Above all, it is a period when reform, real reform of the morality of the clergy, seems incapable

[1] *Storia dell'umanesimo dal XIII al XV secolo*, 3rd ed., Bologna 1947, p. 25.

of achievement, save for the briefest periods and the most restricted localities. What Luther, Calvin and the fathers at Trent accomplished was definition of dogma; pluralism, ignorance, immorality seem as common in all confessions in the seventeenth century as they had been in the undivided Church of the fifteenth. The laymen who were setting the pace in religion were equally setting it in scholarship: the omnivorous honest gentry for whom so many short cuts to universal knowledge were provided, from Pastrengo to Pierre Bayle. For this public the existing university had no relevance as a centre of active scholarship, and consequently in these centuries the universities of Europe enter on a relatively sterile phase of their history.

In literature the period is marked by a striking balance between the new vernaculars and a classical Latin whose revival is discussed in later pages. We are apt to write down the Latin writings produced between the fourteenth and the seventeenth centuries, although practically every important work of scholarship was written in Latin and though its profound influence is still commemorated, at any rate in Europe, in an exceedingly large number of teachers of Latin (who, alas! tend to scorn all the literature written after the second century A.D.). Revived classical Latin gave the vernaculars more than a few merely formal devices: it forced a development of orthography and grammar and vocabulary which might else have taken three or four centuries to accomplish; it gave a characteristic patina to most European literature in the sixteenth and seventeenth centuries. Nor, I believe, is the evidence of art history out of step with the general picture. The late-thirteenth and fourteenth centuries see over all western Europe a new concern for both realism and decoration—the main in-gredients of the 'international Gothic' as the style has been christened. This has its influence even in Italy where another style was to be born destined by the seventeenth century to be accepted throughout the continent, but which spread along paths already in some sense explored, towards destinations already familiar.

Given the secular leadership in religion and literature, given (with the help of Latin) increasingly mature and competent vernaculars, it is not surprising that this period sees a remarkable growth of patriotic sentiment which at times verges on nationalism: the Italians felt themselves superior to the Greeks, let alone to the Barbarians in the north; the French and English began to evolve mythologies about each other; the Germans at Paris objected to being termed the English Nation in the early fifteenth century, while at Constance the claim of Greater Britain to be a leading nation was hotly debated. One characteristic feature which, in different guises, runs through the period from start to finish is known under the name it acquired in the seventeenth century: the Battle of the Books. Yet—and here we are faced with a phenomenon similar to the lay but Christian attitude I have mentioned—this world of separate principates, divided politically and religiously, remained throughout loyal to the old notion of Christen-dom. As Franklin Le Van Baumer has reminded us, Protestant Englishmen rejoiced at the victory of the Papists at Lepanto, and the very word 'Christendom' put up a long fight against its successful rival 'Europe'. Conscious-ness of a larger grouping during the period is, in fact, an amalgam of the two notions, of Europe and of Christendom, similar to the amalgam of town and crown, of land values and cash values, already noted.[1]

When comparison is made with the earlier period, what a different world we find! Christianity then is the business of the clergy, regular and secular. Lay piety has only two distinguishable outward forms—the endowment of the Church and the retreat from the world into the Church. This society, where only clerks were required to be literate, could and did sustain a living Latin literature, but the furtive and despised vernaculars were almost entirely oral. The Latin literature which then flourished was, however, corrupted year by year by contact with inchoate Romance and Teutonic dialects, while a great and fatal division cut across literature: for the serious work was a Latin work and the vernaculars were secular, ephemeral, frivolous; the fine arts, like serious literature, appear almost solely in religious contexts. As against the widely held patriotism I have just mentioned the early middle ages held no loyalties larger than those which sprang from local leadership, except those fugitive and grandiose concepts the Universal Church and the Universal Empire. In such an environment heresy could scarcely flourish, and in fact there is scarcely any before 1200 in the provinces which looked to the Roman pope.

Equally, 'modern' history is cut off, in the matters I have been touching on, from the era that starts in the fourteenth century. As against the widespread but secular interest in Christianity as a moral guide, we have the abandonment of organized religion as an inspiration in the

[1] F. Le Van Baumer's papers, and other related questions, are discussed in my *Europe, The Emergence of an Idea*, Edinburgh 1957, pp. 112–14.

intelligentsia during the nineteenth century. As against the classical norms so universally accepted up to the Enlightenment, and the identification of scholarship with literature, we have romanticism, a subjective approach, a candid specialism in scholarship (aided by the revived Universities), and an encyclopaedism which, unlike its predecessor, caters not for the man who seeks to know all, but for the man who knows he can never know anything. Nationalism, once the decent emotion of responsible men, restricted in scope and elevating in its effects, has become in the last hundred and fifty years the sordid catchword of the masses. Above all, in the modern period proper we are confronted with the universal presence of science. By science today we mean what the earlier period termed Natural Philosophy, and the change in terminology is instructive. For us, all knowledge is essentially scientific in the new sense: our modern heresies are scientific. No doubt the roots of science in this sense go far back: to the Paduan Averroists and Aristotelians, to Ockham's brand of Nominalism, and further still. But we must admit that, before genuinely modern times, science was singularly uninfluential.[1]

Divisions of the seamless web of History, of *durée*, are, I repeat, bound to falsify, for they mean drawing boundaries, however broad and ill-defined, where no

[1] It may perhaps be helpful to note one or two of the criticisms which were made at the time this paper was delivered: Professor M. D. Knowles and the Chairman (Professor W. K. Jordan) considered that the Reformation of the sixteenth century was of more religious significance than I allowed; Dr G. R. Elton felt that monarchy, particularly in England, was an awkward phenomenon to fit into my time-table, and Dr F. Carsten argued the need to give the United Provinces an exceptional place. I must also add that in preparing the original paper I was greatly assisted by several talks with the late Richard Pares.

boundaries were felt to exist at the time: contemporaries at any moment consider themselves to be 'modern'. But for practical purposes such frontiers must be created. No formal discussion of any subject can be conducted save by cutting it up somehow—into courses of lectures or chapters in a book. All that I am urging is that our old twofold division of European history (medieval, modern) should be replaced by a threefold division (medieval, the new period, modern).

Just as the characteristic features of the medieval period—the fief, Gothic architecture, scholastic philosophy—were ultimately to be the pattern for Christendom as a whole but were first and most purely expressed in northern France, so in the succeeding age nearly all that was to be most unique about it was first and most purely expressed in Italy. The morality, the intellectual and artistic styles, and some aspects of politics and economic activity which were in the sixteenth century to provide Europe with a new cultural and social unity, comparable to that of the twelfth century, all these were largely Italian in origin as I hope to show in later pages. Hence it seems not unreasonable to call the new 'middle' ages, the 'late medieval–early modern' of our present arrangements, by the name Renaissance.

In the remainder of this book I shall be considering the origin and development of these new attitudes in Italy, concluding with a brief glance at the adoption of Italian values north of the Alps. That is, I shall be concerned with the Renaissance in Italy and with certain aspects of the Renaissance in Europe at large. But before considering the Italian part of the story which, as I have asserted, is crucial to the general European story, it is necessary to consider carefully the country where these innovations first occurred.

CHAPTER III

THE PROBLEMS OF ITALIAN HISTORY

WHAT do we mean by the history of a country? We mean the way that country has acquired self-consciousness, and the play of interests, political, social, cultural, within the perimeter established by language, by geography and by relations, acquisitive or concessive, with its neighbours. Put like that it sounds very vague indeed. But I think the statement covers Britain, France and many other sovereign states, where a territory, a language, and a tradition of government are all roughly coterminous with accepted or 'natural' frontiers of some kind. It is, of course, true that we falsify the history of England and France in the eleventh and twelfth centuries if we concentrate our attention solely on the ultimate unity. At that time the realities of power were local or at best regional and there was no obvious linguistic or geographical frontier. But the distortion is less damaging in treating England or France than it would be if applied elsewhere, for by the thirteenth century a rough kind of political centralization was effective. This preface is, I feel, worth making before considering the problem of Italian unity.

Since 1870 Italy has been a country with a single more or less sovereign power (my qualification refers to the pope, not to the Republic of San Marino) and its history has been the story of central government, of regional reactions and regional influences within the framework of central government, and of a foreign policy backed by a single national army. No wonder that in preparation for this historians were active in proclaiming Italian unity and no wonder that since 1870 they have been writing Italian history in the way French or English historians write their history. Yet this approach does not in fact correspond with the realities. No history of Italy can be written on the French or British model which does not seriously distort the true picture. Thus, in a sentence, the basic problem of Italian history is that before the nineteenth century there is no Italian history, at least not in the same sense as we talk of English or French history.

The reasons for this are to be sought, in my judgment, partly in the geography of Italy and partly in the accidents of Italian public life. (It will be noted that I am illogically accepting the need to explain the diversity of Italy as though unity were the norm: so powerful is the influence of the model histories of sovereign states.)

The geography of the peninsula is often mentioned by historians. In its historical influence and as the back-cloth for the activities of men and women it is almost *terra incognita*. There is no book devoted to the historical geography of Italy; there is no book dealing systematically with the man-made scenery within the framework of mountain and plain.[1] Yet at every point the clash between natural environment and human activity adds a kind of pathetic grandeur to the Italian scene: the terraces creep

---

[1] Albert von Hofmann, *Das Land Italien und seine Geschichte*, Stuttgart and Berlin 1921, is largely descriptive, concentrates on Roman origins of towns and depends closely on H. Nissen, *Italische Landeskunde*, 2 vols., Berlin 1883–1902, which is restricted to Roman Italy.

up the most unpropitious upper slopes of the hills and one knows that out of sight behind the walls of mountain are the high pastures of summer grazing.

In a sense geography made Italy. The Alps ring the Northern plain and ward off the cold wind and the barbarian, as many a poet has said since Petrarch. But the Alps, formidable as they are, are not a solid wall. Indeed their very formation, with the gentler slopes facing north,

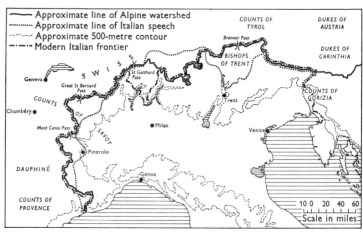

NORTH ITALY: IN THE FOURTEENTH CENTURY AND TODAY

the sharper drop on the Italian side, made them a kind of springboard for attack. The linguistic frontier is a living witness to the ambiguities thus produced and, as we shall see, politics added other denials of this undeniable barrier.

If the Alps and the sea gave Italy a unity, the Apennines went far to cancelling it out. From Lombardy to Sicily the mountains sprawl down the centre of Italy. The country has a spiny back like a fish, said Flavio Biondo.[1] Nor will

[1] *Italia illustrata* in *Opera Omnia*, Basle 1531, p. 294. He had in his mind's eye, without doubt, a contemporary map.

anyone who has flown to Rome or further south in Italy on a fine day readily forget the width of the writhing hills below. As to their height, it is sufficient to say that there is not a square yard of Italy from which one cannot see the uneven border of mountain on at least one skyline.

Yet the hills and mountains descend in Lombardy to a great and fertile plain and elsewhere the land, even the hill land, is sometimes of extraordinary fertility, nourished by volcanic soil and alluvial deposits. The plains thus provided admirable resources for adventurous peoples, while the Alps and the Apennines, with all their sub-ranges, offered ready-made frontiers to attain. Italy was, one might say, condemned to house sharply marked regional groups within its larger entity.

A further point: the depth of the north-south axis of Italy. If Como is only a hundred miles from Berne, the coast of Sicily is only a hundred miles from Tunisia, Otranto is only fifty miles from the coast of Albania.

Naturally, then, Italy has some sharper contrasts than many other lands: contrasts between mountain and plain, between East and West, between North and South. And naturally the diversities thus produced are thus prolonged, finding political expression, sustained by loyalties, fortified by jealousies and suspicions.

This land has none the less known two momentous periods of more or less genuine unity, under the Romans and since 1870. The first was involuntary but lasted some centuries, the second was voluntary and we do not know how long it will last: it is salutary to remember how strongly canvassed has been the notion of regional devolution in Italy in recent years.[1]

It would take too long to survey, however briefly, the course of events in Italy from the period when the Romans acquired control over the whole peninsula down to the moment when Italy was once again a single political unity a hundred years ago. But some points are so central to the story I have to tell that the reader must be reminded of them.

From the Roman period two things must be stressed which were to survive all that the barbarians could do: Roman law and the town. The first survived as the one great source of scholarship in medieval Italy (for the church was no real competitor south of the Alps) and the town of the Romans was the town that was to be reborn in the ninth and tenth centuries. The nucleus of political life in Italy was the town, not (despite the hills) the castle. I know nothing more moving than the sight in most of the bigger Italian towns of the marketing and gossiping which still go on in some space cleared by Roman architects for public activities. I think of that lovely unbroken oval of houses surrounding the piazza del Mercato, once the Roman amphi-theatre, at Lucca [Plate V]; the piazza Erbe at Verona which was once the forum; the piazza Navona at Rome.

---

[1] The constitution which came into effect on 1 January 1948 provided for nineteen regions each of which would have certain representative institutions and functions. Five of these—Sicily, Sardinia, the Valle d'Aosta, Trento–Alto Adige, Friuli–Venezia Giulia—were to have more extensive and separately based powers; of these four are now (1960) functioning; the last named has not yet come into operation. However, one has the impression that public opinion is now tending to turn against the principle of regional autonomy, back to the bold assertion of the commemorative inscription in the Campidoglio where the eternal unity of Italy, proclaimed in 1870, is recorded.

The Problems of Italian History

The centuries following the ending of a Roman empire based on Rome did less damage than the phrases Dark Ages and Barbarian Invasions would suggest. The Ostrogoths came to admire and to emulate; the Lombards had at any rate no alternative civilization to offer. One consequence of Roman grandeur was naturally the attraction exercised on the barbarians by the motherland of wealth and power: they came to enjoy and only incidentally to damage. Nevertheless whatever effective unity the Romans had made of Italy was destroyed and all that remained of it was a papacy, at once victim and exploiter of the lords of Italy and the emperor at Byzantium. The living world of Rome was now the eastern Empire and from Ravenna slowly spread the architectural and artistic forms which were to be regarded for long in Italy as models of propriety and devotion. The public life of Italy was now totally decentralized, and so it was to remain for a millennium. Indeed for centuries the seats of real power were to multiply until by the thirteenth century the map of the peninsula resembled the jigsaw puzzle of Germany. There are, alas, no scholarly Italian historical atlases. Perhaps we have in this fractionalization a partial excuse.[1]

Not that there was in this long period no consolidation. The papal states emerge, curious testimony to the logic of the Apennines, with a northern section to the east of the watershed (Romagna and the March of Ancona), a southern section to the west (the later Patrimony and Campagna) and a turbulent bridge between them through the shrunken Duchy of Spoleto. South of that a Norman

---

[1] The best maps of medieval Italy are those by T. Menke in Spruner und Menke, *Historischer Hand-Atlas*, 3rd ed., Gotha 1880.

kingdom had replaced the Lombards in the mainland and the Moslems in Sicily. But these larger political groupings were often a mere veneer over the little communities and the local lords who enjoyed genuine independence. And in Tuscany and Lombardy, in the Northern Apennines and in the foot-hills of the Alps a bewildering variety of separate jurisdictions were maintained.

The issue which from time to time subsumed the lowlier rivalries was, of course, the struggle of the popes to free themselves from the control of German emperors and to prevent any other prince from exercising power in Italy. The upshot was the imposition on both parties of the realities of the situation. Subject to a respect for the forces of law, for the residual power of the emperor in the North, for the pope in centre and South, the thirteenth century witnesses a self-conscious liberty in the communes where the flowering of commercial activity had brought wealth and a desire to be rid of old controls. The ports of Italy were carrying an ever larger trade. Two non-Roman towns are symbols of the new urban life: Venice had grown up on its insalubrious marsh independent of both pope and emperor; and in 1168 the Lombard League founded Alessandria, a gesture defying the emperor.

Unhappily neither pope nor emperor readily accepted these developments. The popes drove the Hohenstauffen out of Naples by invoking the Angevins; a Catalan conquest of Sicily gave Aragon an interest in Italy; and the emperors resumed their intervention when Henry VII descended into Italy in 1310, hailed by Dante, a pathetic figure or a romantic figure as one pleases, but by any reckoning an ineffective and misguided prince.

The Problems of Italian History

This episode, so far as its date is concerned, ushers in the Renaissance period of Italian history, which I propose to discuss in greater detail in later pages. With regard to the pattern of Italian politics the fourteenth and fifteenth centuries saw no real change. It is true that imperial intervention became merely ludicrous and that the absence of the popes at Avignon followed by the schism provided a century when no real opposition was placed by the papacy in the way of the plans of Robert of Anjou or Ladislas in Naples, or of the Visconti lords of Milan. But the ambitions of these men encountered resistance from other centres of power and so bitter was the conflict that it even led, in the Peace of Lodi (1454) and the convention which followed it, to an attempt to substitute arbitration for war. This could not succeed. Italian princes and towns continued the old way of seeking outside help and this ended in the French intervention of 1494. Once again Northern princes were involved in securing the prizes of the divided peninsula. The rulers of the early sixteenth century were, however, not the small dynasts of Anjou or Aragon: it was a new and united France, a new and united Spain which fought over Italy and in the end destroyed her independence between 1527 and 1559. Only with Napoleon was the foreign hegemony seriously disturbed; only with the mid-nineteenth century did the Italians rule their own land.

I have felt bound to recall these events, for without remembering how divided Italy was one cannot understand either the true history of the country or the place in it of the Renaissance. How may the historian dealing with Italy prior to 1800 discuss regions, towns, families—where real power lay—within some kind of a framework which will not impose on them a quite factitious homogeneity?

Nothing shows the difficulty better than what Italians did about it themselves. Northern European countries have a historiographical tradition which throws the Italian dilemma into sharp relief. The Anglo-Saxon Chronicle, Malmesbury, the St Albans writers down to Matthew Paris were, whether they knew it or not, writing the history of England. A *de gestis regum Angliae* was a history of England because of the king's interests in, and often effective control over, most of the country. And so, in a less marked fashion, with France. But no works like this can be found in Italy:[1] only in dealing with the Lombard invasions do the medieval chroniclers and subsequent writers tell a national story. The Italian chronicler was amazingly precocious. From the start of the eleventh century the Italian communes began to acquire historians. But their work is securely founded on a locality, and whatever Salimbene did it was not to write the history of Italy. However important and general the events which are related may be, they are seen partially. So Albertino Mussato saw Henry VII and the aftermath of his expeditions from the Paduan point of view; so the Villanis saw Italy and the world from Florence.

It is, in fact, not until the mid-fifteenth century that we come upon two writers who, the one more or less explicitly, the other more or less implicitly, make Italy the centre of the story. One cannot, as I have tried to show

[1] I think the only general work is still U Balzani, *Early Chroniclers of Europe: Italy*, London 1883.

elsewhere,[1] treat the *Decades* of Flavio Biondo as simply a history of Italy, just as it is demonstrably not a history of Christendom or Europe. One might say it begins as the latter and ends as the former. And we should ponder his desperate complaints when faced from 1400 or thereabouts with the intricacies of divided Italy.[2] The annals he compiled were the annals of wars and diplomacy; internal history is neglected and we can learn next to nothing from the *Decades* of the rise of the Medici, the waning powers of the Doge. The ambiguity of the *Decades* is reflected in its vague title and we might hope for more from that equally neglected and even more original book by Biondo, the *Italia illustrata*. Here we have Italy literally laid on a map before us: the eighteen provinces[3] which he describes are not only a reminder of the many units in which sovereignty was exercised,[4] but at the outset he says that it is his aim to give not only a description of Italy, but also a compendium of Italian history. If we look to see what this means we find a very odd situation: all that is of general significance seems to be hooked on to the province of Romagna. There we find an outline of the revival of letters under the inspiration of Giovanni of Ravenna—who has given so much trouble to later historians. And there we find a retrospective account of Italian history, which may be summarized as follows.[5]

---

[1] 'The *Decades* of Flavio Biondo', *Proc. Br. Acad.* XLV (1959), 97–128.

[2] Cf. *ibid.* p. 109.

[3] Sicily and the other islands are not included; nor is Piedmont. A critical edition of this work, at which Biondo continued to work after its publication, is urgently needed.

[4] This is, of course, not how they are distinguished; nor were there only eighteen centres of power.

[5] *Italia illustrata*, pp. 345–8.

After the Republic and the Empire came four hundred years of invasion by barbarians. This was followed by a century of peace under Charlemagne and his successors followed by wretchedness with the tyranny of Berengar. There followed a period when Italy enjoyed varying fortune under the rule of the emperors. Even the worst periods of imperial rule were, however, less disastrous than the internal divisions within Italy which then developed. The country was divided against itself and at this stage several cities in Lombardy and in the march of Treviso established their liberty and buttressed it by alliances with each other. Then on the one side came the emperors Otto III, Henry III, Henry IV, Henry VII and Lewis of Bavaria to challenge pope and people on the other side: the result was a time of terrible affliction—fire, sacking, death and shame; more terrible by far than the time of barbarian attack. Faced with impending ruin the popes and some of the cities sought the support of foreign countries to drive out the crowd of Germans, and so came into Italy as hired soldiers the French, Spaniards, English and Bretons. From Martin IV to Gregory XI the Italians paid foreign mercenaries, themselves taking no pay, but fighting as a matter of honour. However, these foreign troops often did more harm than the enemies they were sent against: Perugia, Cesena and Faenza are witnesses to this and so are the lands round Rome which have still not yet recovered. It was in these conditions that the Visconti rose to power, aided by Benedict XII against Lewis of Bavaria. They contracted with Alberico da Barbiano against the French and English. Nearly always victorious, Alberico became captain of the Company of St George, from which descended all the great Italian captains. Alberico then served Ladislas of Naples, who established himself so firmly throughout Italy that he would, but for his premature death, undoubtedly have acquired the title of emperor. This expulsion of foreigners and founding of generations of Italian military leaders was the reason for Italy becoming more prosperous. For in subsequent wars, when the ultramontanes were gone, if cities were sacked they were not at any rate put to fire and the sword, and in the fighting what one Italian lost was gained at least by another Italian; and indeed at this stage Italy was exporting her captains to foreign countries and the wealth there obtained by them came back still further to enrich the motherland and encourage the modern fashion of rich dress and splendid buildings. The return of the court from Avignon to Rome also made for opulence and high living.

Now some of this has a familiar ring about it: bits of it have become embedded in the tradition of Italian historiography.[1] But my immediate point is to recall where it is introduced into the *Italia illustrata*. It comes under 'Romagna'. And the peal of praise for Alberico da Barbiano, as earlier for John of Ravenna, is really praise for the province of Biondo himself. He makes the point in no uncertain way: eloquence came to Italy from John of Ravenna, a better sort of warfare from Alberico, and 'Romagna has given Italy its third glory when I wrote my history, restored Rome, as now I am illustrating Italy'.[2] This extraordinary mixture of the parochial and the broad

[1] Especially the descent of Sforza and Braccio from the army of Alberico.
[2] Biondo is referring to his *Decades*, his *Roma instaurata* and the present *Italia illustrata*.

view exactly fixes the ablest Renaissance attempt to view Italy as a unit.

The other work I mentioned, which implicitly dealt with Italy as a whole, is Platina's *Lives of the Popes*. In a sense this, like Biondo's *Decades*, begins with Christendom and ends with Italy, for this was what happened to the papacy. But by the time Platina wrote it (1472–4) the popes no longer had truly Italian aims. They were princes like the rest, uneasily protecting themselves and the families on whom they depended for political support, by whom they were exploited during the period of their plenitude of power. As a result the picture of Italian politics which we find in Platina is even more confused than the contemporary portion of the *Decades* of Biondo. Both writers thus testify to the uncoordinated Italian scene; both reflect the absence of a really Italian story.

After these blundering attempts to write the history of Italy[1] it is with astonishment that one encounters the truly remarkable *Storia d'Italia* of Guicciardini. Here we have a detached analysis of the political development of the peninsula written with a maturity and a cogency which make Biondo, Platina and indeed all earlier and many later historians seem incompetent and amateurish. It was to be perhaps the most influential work in fixing the approach and content of later historical writing in the contemporary field and it has laid its imprint with devastating finality on all later interpretations of Italian history. Yet three important qualifications must be made before we jump to the conclusion that for Italian historians the way forward was now clear. First, Guicciardini's book was not

[1] Sabellico's *Enneades* (1498–1504) is really an elaboration of Biondo's *Decades* from a Venetian standpoint.

published, and that partially, till over twenty years after he died in 1540, and in Italy the complete text did not appear until the early nineteenth century;[1] that is to say, we must guard against assuming that the work had the effect on contemporaries that it has on us, however popular it was when it appeared. Second, and following from this, Guicciardini had in fact no true successors in the field of Italian history for centuries: his book is better regarded as the culmination of a process rather than the beginning of one. And third, the *Storia d'Italia* is not a general history of Italy from the start to his own day. It is the history of about forty years, from 1492 to 1532. Now these years see, as Guicciardini put it, 'le calamità d'Italia', when Italy having enjoyed a period of unparalleled prosperity collapses before the French and then the other foreign armies whose presence in Italy had been solicited by Italians themselves. It is the story of a nemesis; it has the unity of a tragedy. But it offered no formula for treating Italian history as a whole. Italian history of the periods before 1492 and after the Spanish domination had been secured remained, despite Guicciardini, at the regional level.

It was the merit of the later antiquarians to accept this. Scores of histories of towns and principalities are to be found in the later-sixteenth, seventeenth and eighteenth centuries. The industrious compilers of historical methods of the early Enlightenment could list a hundred pages of titles dealing with provincial Italy but only two of titles of general works.[2] 'We are obliged with all these particular

---

[1] *Ed. princeps*, Florence–Venice 1561, 1564; ed. Rosini, 1820.
[2] See R. Rawlinson's version of Langlet du Fresnoy, *A New Method of Studying History*, etc., 2 vols., London 1728, II, 338–41, 341–437.

histories', wrote one such eighteenth-century scholar, 'to supply the defect of a general Italian history...the Italians are rich in the particular stories of their different states, but want a perfect body of history.'[1] Far and away the best of the few general works appeared at this very time.[2] Muratori, towards the end of a long life of exemplary labour and erudition, published his *Annali d'Italia*. The work came out in two parts. The first nine volumes fulfilled his original plan of covering the Christian era down to 1500; they were published in 1744. The remaining three volumes run from 1500 to 1747, the year of their publication. Muratori knew the narrative sources of Italian history better than any man before or since: portions of his *Scriptores* are still indispensable. The *Annali* do no more and no less than assemble the facts from these narrative sources. In our sense they are not a history, and this is all the truer of the critical centuries from 1300 to 1500. Restricted as he obliged himself to be to the *civil* history of Italy (for he felt that Baronius and Ughelli had treated the church sufficiently fully[3]) he lacked even the slender thread of coherence that the papal story afforded after the destruction of the empire in the thirteenth century. And so, year by year, Muratori gives us the events in different parts of Italy, not a rationalized account of Italy as a whole. Only when

---

[1] Rawlinson, *op. cit.* I, 145; the second sentence is quoted from Rapin.

[2] Of the others we may note C. Sigonio's two works which, on the pattern of Biondo but with a surer sense of documentary sources, conflate the annals of Italy from A.D. 284 to 1268. Sigonio died in 1584. See E. Fueter, trs. Jeanmaire, *Histoire de l'histoire moderne*, pp. 158–9. Of his predecessors Muratori regarded Sigonio as the only one worth mentioning: *Annali*, I, prefazione.

[3] C. Baronius, *Annales ecclesiastici*, Rome 1588–1607; F. Ughelli, *Italia Sacra*, Rome 1643–62.

he comes under the spell of Guicciardini does the compilation reach the general—for the invasion of 1494 and the wars that follow.[1] Thereafter if his patterns are simpler the explanation is that Italy had fewer independent states and none that sought actively to disturb the situation. His own relief at this is undisguised:

Anyone alive today [he wrote in 1744] must raise his hands to heaven and thank God to be born in this century rather than earlier. In earlier days we can find an occasional good prince, some few days of peace, of magnificence and delight; nor can one deny that Italy in the past was richer than today. But taking the picture as a whole the comparison is: then cruel tyrants, now beneficent rulers; then wars of lawless brutality, sackings and burnings and all manner of wantonness, now when wars do occur they are conducted by men who respect their Christian obligations and in fact we enjoy an enviable peace; then the horrors of Guelf and Ghibelline, now we have gone far even to reduce the volume of the other infliction, the Plague....Compared with all others our century is a blessed one.[2]

I have lingered a moment with Muratori, for soon after him the entire picture changes. The doctrine of liberty and nationalism is proclaimed in France; the armies of Napoleon destroy the Italy established in 1559. Two generations follow in the peninsula whose aim is simply the unification and emancipation of their country. The old acceptance of the variety of states is swept away. The history of Italy must be written in a new manner.

First in the field was the Swiss writer Sismondi. His *Histoire des républiques Italiennes du moyen âge* appeared in sixteen volumes between 1809 and 1818. It is the history

[1] *Annali*, IX, 570–606; X, 1–403.
[2] *Ibid.* IX, *ad fin.*

of the rise and fall of liberty in Italy. Liberty and greatness go together; the achievements of the Italians, and the Renaissance above all, are the product of communal independence; only a federation could save this; failure to federate meant French invasion, Spanish occupation, political and cultural mediocrity. This is the *message* of Sismondi: it is belied in the detailed complexity of his narrative, for he was a good and faithful scholar and stuck closely to the paths hacked out in the jungle by Biondo, Sigonio and Muratori, paths which mostly led far away from his central theme.

Sismondi had Italian blood in his veins, but the cause of Italian unity as a practical issue did not move him as it stirred the Italians themselves, who, faced with the hope of liberty and national independence, realized how urgently they needed a history of Italy. And so emerged what Croce has called the 'poem', picking the word from an essay by one of the advocates of unity—Cesare Balbo.[1] Some fine fragments came out of this patriotic urge, though not the awaited history, and a violent quarrel over the place of the pope in the story dissipated scholarship in polemics.[2]

Italian unity was achieved. Technical historical scholarship of German origin spread in Italy as it spread elsewhere. Historical journals multiplied and so did university institutes and learned monographs. All of this was contained, so to speak, within the concept of a united Italy, but no sweeping survey came such as De Sanctis provided for Italian

[1] Balbo, *Pensieri sulla storia d'Italia*, quoted B. Croce, *Storia della storiografia italiana nel secolo decimonono*, 3rd ed., 2 vols., Bari 1947, I, 108.

[2] Cf. Croce's chapters on the neo-Guelfs and neo-Ghibellines, *ibid.* I, 120–207; a brief but detached comment in Gooch, *History and Historians in the Nineteenth Century*, London 1913, pp. 434–40.

literature: indeed when De Sanctis died in 1883 he was generally dismissed as brilliant but essentially unscholarly.[1] The answer to the demand for a history covering the whole of the national past was, in Italy as in France, Germany and Britain, felt to be best provided in collaborative works.

Just how currently awkward the question of writing Italian history can be is illustrated from a good example of this type of manual—the work of Luigi Simeoni, *Le Signorie*.[2] This is the latest version of the earlier surveys by Carlo Cipolla published in 1881[3] [cf. above, p. vi] and by Pietro Orsi, published in 1900.[4] All of these come from the same publishing house.[5] We may note sadly that the 'society of friends' responsible for the series in which Cipolla's volume appeared, the 'society of professors' which produced Orsi's work,[6] has been replaced in our own day merely by a group of 'collaborators'. Cipolla's very elaborate and Orsi's briefer study are traditional in their form: all regional issues are subsumed in a single 'Italian' narrative.[7] Simeoni's study, which runs from 1313 to 1559, is not like this and is quite unlike any hand-book

[1] Croce, *Storia della storiografia*, II, 58–9.   [2] 2 vols., Milan 1950.
[3] *Storia delle signorie italiane dal 1313 al 1530.*   [4] *Signorie e principati.*
[5] Vallardi.   [6] See the amusing lines of Croce on this: *op. cit.* II, 62.
[7] Cipolla's volume, very fully annotated with references to the older collections of sources, is still useful. The original paper cover (bound in vol. I of the London Library copy) is worth looking at [above, p. vi]. Round the frame run medallions with the pictures of heroes of an *Italian* historiography, together with symbols of the main towns (not, be it noted, provinces): there is no Italian symbol, though we have ROMA in capitals. Of the historians depicted the three likely to be unfamiliar to the English reader are: Pietro Verri (1728–97), author of *Meditazioni sull'economia politica*; Carlo Denina (1731–1813), author of *Istoria delle revoluzioni d'Italia* and other works; Carlo Botta (1766–1837), author of *Storia d'Italia*.

In Cipolla's own introduction he refers to Cesare Balbo, 'la cui stupenda divisione della storia italiana fu presa a base della pubblicazione di cui il presente libro è un anello'.

to English or French history. This is partly because the church and ecclesiastical history are completely ignored: the pope figures solely as an Italian prince. Partly it is because artistic and intellectual history are also omitted: one could hardly infer from Simeoni that a revival of letters and art had taken place. But most notably and on the political level Simeoni has really written two books: one on Italy and one on the Italian provinces. He surveys the fourteenth century from the Italian point of view in several chapters, and then turns to discuss in separate chapters the history of Venice, Lombardy, Piedmont, Genoa, Tuscany and so on. And similarly he deals with the fifteenth century and again the first half of the sixteenth. This sounds an attractive approach and indeed it is better (to my mind) than the alternative of forcing all local issues into a general story, even if that story covers ideas, art and religion, as in Nino Valeri's recent and very attractive book.[1] There is no doubt that power and politics in Italy were regional, and only seldom reached a critical moment in which the peninsula as a whole was involved.[2] My criticism of Simeoni would be that his general chapters are often concerned with regional issues; that his regional chapters do not deal with many of the smaller but real units of Italian life. The whole political organization of the mountain areas is virtually ignored: what of the chameleon-like Malaspina who survived for centuries in the no-man's-land between Liguria, Tuscany and Lombardy? And even on the plain the lesser lords who trimmed so successfully

[1] *L'Italia nell'età dei principati dal 1343 al 1516*, Verona 1950.
[2] Cf. Hans Baron, *Crisis of the Early Italian Renaissance*, Princeton, 2 vols., 1955, II, 387–90, where Simeoni is criticized, Valeri praised.

to maintain their independence, the smaller urban communities who were in practice allowed much liberty by their masters are passed over without a word, or figure merely as adhering to a treaty between the bigger powers. To all this the learned author could retort that I am demanding the impossible. This is true. But it is equally true that Italian history is only slightly less distorted by treating as basic the so-called 'great powers' of the peninsula; or by creating (though this can have valuable results) a series of regional groupings.[1] What matters to most men is local freedom, prestige and power in their own community. It is not till the sixteenth century that Italian courts exercise the kind of magnetism which reduces to the parochial the urban and rural centres pivoting round Rome, Venice, Naples and Milan. The truth of the fourteenth and fifteenth century is so localized as not to be comprehended in a simple collection of studies of large provinces, let alone a single Italian narrative. Dante's estimate that in his day there were more than a thousand varieties of the vernacular 'in hoc minimo mundi angulo' might equally be applied to the political divisions as well.[2]

There was, moreover, in most communities a deep cleavage between nobility, merchants and the *minuto popolo*. Government of old had been nominally in the hands of the imperial vicar or *podestà*, the nominated representative of the pope, the officials appointed by the king in Naples. The thirteenth century saw everywhere the real power in the hands of locally chosen magistrates,

[1] See the very interesting brief article by Giacomo Devoto, 'Per la storia delle regioni d'Italia', *Rivista storica italiana*, LXXII (1960), 221–33.
[2] *De vulg. eloqu.* I, X, 9.

and town councils emerge which reflect roughly the divergent interests of the two main sections, the *grandi* (nobles) and the *grassi* (wealthy merchants): the small fry of the town were mere make-weights in the struggle. Even in the towns of the *regno*, backward and feudal Naples, we find statutes providing for the representation of merchant and magnate. In Tuscany and Lombardy the opposed groups in the later thirteenth century were without any real check and in consequence a constant friction resulted in the field of urban taxation, a friction which was in the fourteenth and fifteenth centuries to bring about the ending of communal government almost everywhere. So that to the complexities already instanced must be added the turmoil of faction within the urban community. Nor was it a simple class issue—noble Ghibellines *versus* merchant Guelfs. The Ghibellines were divided between themselves and nobles often found themselves supporting merchant policies. There are many moments when the outcome of a crisis turns on the temper of a quarter of a city, a street or a clan.

In the picture I have tried to sketch of the problem of Italian unity, which (as will readily be seen) could have political overtones in the Fascist period,[1] the Renaissance has an important role both as a period of time and as a cultural movement. As a period of time it represents those two centuries, from roughly 1330 to 1530, when Italy became, what France had been and was again to be, the intellectual and artistic pacemaker of Europe; at the same

[1] When some Italians tried to make any questioning of the fundamental unity of Italy a police matter. See B. Croce, 'Recenti controversie intorno all' unità della storia d'Italia', *Proc. Br. Acad.* XXII (1936).

time it is a period when the political life of the peninsula slowly lost its vigour, to succumb to foreign occupation. As for the cultural movement, were its roots native, was it the cause or the consequence of internal division, did the country pay too great a price for being 'the first-born among the sons of modern Europe'?[1] Above all, how far did the very concept of rebirth, the renaissance sentiment itself, contribute to the dilemma of unity and diversity? To what extent did the consciousness of Italy as homogeneous, the product of shared experiences, emerge as a consequence of the Renaissance? These are questions which will occupy us later and which cannot be divorced from either the particularism I have so far insisted upon, nor from certain unifying features of the peninsula which I wish to consider in the concluding pages of this chapter.

Certain features of the Italian scene do transcend the turbulence and the fragmentation, though we must handle them discreetly if we are to avoid over-estimating their significance.

First we must recognize those two fundamental aspects of the Italian scene to which I have already referred: towns and the law. No other part of Europe witnessed such a remarkable urban development. In no other part of Europe did law, civil and canon, play so large a part in the life of the community. Both, as we shall see, contributed to the emergence of a society more secular in orientation than we find elsewhere; both provide assumptions, political and social and intellectual, which are common to all parts of the peninsula.

[1] Burckhardt's phrase.

Next I place religion and the church. These are quite separate often, but the second was occasionally closely connected with the former. The northerner must be wary of his reactions to Italian religion and I do not wish to do more than suggest that its passion, its prophecies and its appeal to the senses have a kind of coherence both when compared with northern Europe and also internally. Take the saints. Within the period covered in this book, mid-fourteenth to mid-sixteenth century, some eighty-two individuals in Italy were added to the 125 to whom this supreme recognition had been accorded in the preceding 150 years. Over two hundred Italian saints in three and a half centuries, compared with sixty for France in the same period, twenty-six for Spain and even fewer elsewhere.[1] Now it may be the case that Italian popes (so far as they were responsible for beatification) would sympathize with such expressions of devotion by their fellow-countrymen more readily than by non-Italians: but we must note that while the popes were at Avignon, all Frenchmen and out of Italy, only some ten French saints were recognized compared with about forty-six Italian saints. The point is surely that the pressure for saints was greater in Italy, even if saintly persons were no commoner. Beatification was, I suggest, an assertion of a kind of patriotism rooted in a local cult, but linking the saint and his locality with a larger community not merely hereafter but here below. There was then, as there is today, no other Italian Pantheon. Then, as now, the tribute of the church, expressed by the pope, was for Italians the highest possible

[1] These very rough and ready figures are calculated from the lists in H. Mas-Latrie, *Trésor de chronologie*, Paris 1889.

earthly gesture. It is sobering to recall recent moves to secure the beatification of Savonarola and gossip (it seems to be no more) about a process for Manzoni. Was not Commynes told by an Italian 'Nous appellons, en ce païs icy, sainctz tous ceulx qui nous font du bien'?[1] Was not Boccaccio's most famous tale his first, where the rogue Ser Cepparello da Prato was transmogrified into the San Ciappelletto of holy repute? And do we not read elsewhere in the *Decameron* of the holidays of Ravenna where a saint and his cult existed for every day in the year?[2]

If Italy was then a land of saints it was also a land of clergy. Biondo tells us that the curia reckoned that there were 264 episcopal sees, and this seems to be in fact a slight underestimate.[3] This is almost as many as we can find in all the other countries of western Christendom put together and is a factor in Italian history with an influence not yet adequately recognized, for if the northern sees, in Lombardy, Piedmont, Venetia, were reasonably large, in central and southern Italy they were tiny, often poor and thus tightly dependent on the pope rather than on a great family, and sufficiently adroit to weather unscathed the crisis of the sixteenth century. Here I introduce them merely as a symbol of the large number of secular clergy in the peninsula. But to these we must add an even larger number

[1] The man, a native of Borgo San Siro (near Pavia), was referring to Gian-galeazzo: Commynes, *Mémoires*, ed. Calmette, III, 58. Sacchetti called his fellow-countrymen idolaters: *Trecento novelle*, ed. V. Pernicone, Florence 1946, no. CLVII, p. 377.

[2] *Dec.* I, i; II, x (see V. Branca's note, I, 296).

[3] *Italia illustrata*, p. 295; in Eubel, *Hierarchia catholica*, I, I count sixty-four sees in North Italy, sixty-five in central Italy (not including Rome), and 137 in south Italy—a total of 266 (in addition there were eleven in Sicily, eighteen in Sardinia and six in Corsica); the total for Germany, France, Spain, Portugal England and Scotland is 267.

of regulars in a bewildering number of orders, sub-orders and congregations, all striving for papal favour.[1]

Positively therefore religious sentiment and a huge number of clergy acted as a kind of cement in Italy. Equally cohesive, it appears to me, was the reverse of this, an anti-clerical attitude in the masses and in governments, a rigid pressure against the clergy.

The existence of anti-clerical sentiment in every part of medieval Christendom is, of course, a basic fact which only too often tends to be overlooked or smothered by the equally undoubted faith of the masses. Anti-clericalism in a sense is only possible to true believers. The church satisfies their spiritual craving; the clergy inflame their hatred and contempt. We are in no doubt about the veneration of the priest at the altar; let us not forget the odium and suspicion he attracted when he crossed the threshold into the market-place.[2] Dante's attitude is, after all, just this contempt for pope and priest, just this reverence for church and creed; Marsilio knew his Dante and there are pages in the *Defensor pacis* to which Dante himself would have subscribed.[3] At a lower and, in a way, a more important level (for how singularly ineffective were the attacks on theocracy of both Dante and Marsilio)

[1] At Florence in the early fourteenth century the clergy seem to have formed about three per cent of the population: see J. Beloch's discussion of the famous passage in G. Villani, XI, 93: *Bevölkerungsgeschichte Italiens*, II (Berlin 1940) pp. 129–30; the number for England in 1377 has been put at 1·5% by J. C. Russell, *Brit. Med. Population*, Albuquerque 1948, p. 145. Numbers of Italian clergy, regular and secular, are highest in the early eighteenth century. Was the rise steady during the fifteenth, sixteenth and seventeenth centuries?

[2] Cf. the excellent pages of Joseph Bédier, *Les Fabliaux*, 2nd ed., Paris 1895, pp. 311, 332–40; the consistent pillorying of the religious is neither reforming nor irreligious, nor satirical.

[3] The *Defensor Pacis* was first translated into Tuscan at Florence in 1363.

anti-clericalism meets us everywhere in popular sources from the thirteenth century onwards. One might hazard the guess that the hatred of the Italian clergy was in pro-portion to their prominence in every community in Italy. It was naturally intensified by charges of pluralism, ignor-ance, immorality, many of which seem well-founded; each order accused its rivals of vice and corruption; all orders preached against the secular clergy. And a radical-heretical strain of criticism is found all over the country in the Fraticelli.

Official policy towards the church in the Italian state was completely in line with the jealous behaviour familiar to us in England and France, and just as important. It is, therefore, a matter for regret that so little worth while has been written on church–state relations in medieval Italy.[1] As Volpe pointed out, church and secular powers both reached a stage of self-conscious independence about 1200, when the full Gregorian doctrine was applied by lawyer popes like Innocent III, and the commune arises in the north and centre as a genuine focus of authority.[2] The result was a series of bitter struggles in every part of the peninsula: in the south between the church and Frederick II, taking forms more nearly comparable with those in the kingdoms of northern Europe, and in Tuscany, Lombardy, Emilia and Venetia between the church and individual communes. The subjects of dispute are those one would

---

[1] I have come on only two sensible essays, G. Salvemini's 'Le lotte fra stato chiesa nei comuni italiani durante il secolo XIII', reprinted in his *Studi storici*, Florence 1901, pp. 39–90; and C. Volpe, 'Chiesa e stato di città nell'Italia medievale', *Medio evo italiano*, 2nd ed., Florence 1928, pp. 197–214. The sub-ject has attracted a large, but mainly polemical, literature. Much of value has, of course, been written on the *political* struggles between particular popes and particular towns and princes. [2] *Op. cit.* pp. 198–9.

expect: clerical claims to jurisdictional and financial immunities, tithes, mortmain, and control of appointment to benefices. What is striking is the ruthless way in which the commune proceeded against the clergy. In protecting a civil litigant, for instance, all the clergy in a commune were the subject of reprisals.[1] If a church court refused to prosecute a clerical defendant, lay courts occasionally 'imprisoned the guilty clerks, tried them and executed them'.[2] The statutes of the Capitano and Podestà at Florence in 1322–5 combine all the rigours of the Constitutions of Clarendon and the statutes of Provisors and Praemunire: any man who did not accept the civil jurisdiction of the commune was normally to be outlawed; no subject of the commune could be cited before any court outside the commune; the lay relatives of clerical offenders were to be held responsible for such offences; it was an offence to seek and obtain an excommunication or an interdict; no church court could delay let alone suspend the judgment of a lay tribunal; no man might appeal from a lay court to a church court; and so on.[3] Clerical sanctions, such as the use of interdict, were met by compelling the clergy to perform divine office under threat of outlawry. The activities of the inquisition were, though related to faith and not to the disputed borderline legal and financial matters I have mentioned, frequently the occasion of violent popular reactions.[4] We must not over-emphasize the successes of the lay government. Save at Venice,[5] the

[1] Salvemini, *op. cit.* p. 46.
[2] *Ibid.* p. 45.   [3] *Ibid.* pp. 77–8.
[4] As at Parma in 1279, when the Dominican convent was sacked after the burning of two heretic women, *ibid.* p. 88.
[5] *Ibid.* p. 48.

clergy managed to maintain at any rate their theoretical exemption from direct taxation; and the fiercer laws, like the Florentine statutes of 1322–5, were often softened in practice. But the fact remains that from top to bottom Italy saw a consistent and on the whole effective assertion of the right of the civil magistrate to control the clergy. The *pars principativa* (to quote Marsilio of Padua) had mastered the *pars sacerdotalis* and the effort transcends and unites the several and often warring towns and principalities of Italy. In this at least Ghibelline and Guelf were at one; whatever their attitude to the pope, they were of one mind as regards the clergy.[1]

Religious sentiment, an obtrusive clergy and an anti-clericalism of sentiment and political practice were not more important in uniting the Italians of the middle ages than trade. We are accustomed to thinking of Italian trade in terms of what the French call 'le grand commerce', a long-distance trade in commodities and services which ranged from the North Sea and the Baltic to the Middle East and beyond. We should, however, remember that there was a very considerable internal trade in Italy.[2] The geographical diversity of the peninsula, its mountains and its plains, its northern portion touching central Europe, its southern portion almost reaching Africa, all made for a

[1] See the violent anti-clerical legislation of the Ghibellines at Parma which was maintained when control passed in 1247 to the Guelfs, *ibid.* p. 86.

[2] For Italian economic history the best general survey, with bibliographies, is G. Luzzatto, *Storia economica d'Italia*, I (all published), *L'antichità e il medioevo*, Rome 1949. Hearty agreement must be expressed with his remarks, pp. 265–7, on the need for more to be done on agrarian history, neglected in the interest of urban, industrial and commercial history, on which there are many useful studies. I have to thank Dr Philip Jones for allowing me to read the manuscript of his chapter on Italian medieval agrarian history written for the new edition of the *Cambridge Econ. Hist.* vol. I.

certain reciprocity in the production of essential commodities. Self-sufficiency was doubtless the aim of each community, but the nature of the country, and above all the development of large manufacturing centres in the towns of the centre and north, prevented it from happening. 'The result was trade between "industrial" and "agrarian" Italy, whereby agricultural regions like Piedmont, the Ferrarese, most of peninsular Italy and the islands offered farm produce for money and manufactures.' Above all, in the basic commodity, corn, the south supplied the north: Sicily, Apulia, Sardinia regularly sold their surpluses to the Tuscan and Lombard towns.[2] Beyond this unifying effect of intra-Italian trade, one's impression is that the most fully exploited market of Italian businessmen was Italy itself. The Bardi, for instance, whom one thinks of in connection with Florentine adventure in distant lands, had as many branches in Italian towns as they had outside Italy. The precocious Italian merchant, I am trying to suggest (it is no more than a suggestion), though in terms of Italy first and then beyond. With the whole of Europe to choose from, L. B. Alberti makes Lionardo in the *Della famiglia* suggest only Italian towns as offering a sufficient choice of climates for the promotion of health.[3]

The bigger Italian towns were thronged by merchants

[1] Dr Jones, *op. cit.*, who points out, however, that the 'agrarian' Alpine valleys had to import grain, the 'industrial' Milanese could sometimes export it; and cf. Luzzatto, pp. 318–20. Oil and salt were also important commodities in trade within Italy.

[2] Cf. R. Romano, 'A propos du commerce du blé dans la méditerranée des XIVe et XVe siècles', *Éventail de l'histoire vivante* [à Lucien Febvre] 2 vols., Paris 1953, pp. 149–61. In connection with Italian internal trade one would like to know more about the fairs of Italy; cf. Luzzatto, pp. 324–5.

[3] *Della Famiglia*, ed. F. C. Pellegrini and R. Spongano, Florence 1946, p. 177.

from other parts of Italy: they were also often linked to the rest of the peninsula by a different type of visitor. The punishment of exile was an ancient one, which was applied with a ruthlessness and an irresponsibility beyond any Roman precedents in and after the thirteenth century. We know a good deal about the diffusion of the practice and the legal sanctions it involved within the Italian sovereign community;[1] and we know a great deal about the history of some illustrious exiles, notably Dante. But about *fuoruscitismo* (the *utilis et necessaria quotidiana materia de bannitis*, as the lawyer Nello de San Geminiano, *fl. c.* 1400, called it) we know very little indeed and can only guess at its consequences. These were clearly of great importance in determining the ups and downs of policy in many towns, Florence, Genoa, Bologna and so on; they were not insignificant in determining the course of events in 1494. They were, I think, of larger import even than this. 'Rebellare' in Italian is a transitive verb, and this alone suggests how important the exiles were in the politics of every town and region. The treatment of exiles was a matter for negotiation between governments. Exile spread the most active political figures round the towns and courts of Italy, and, being out of office and thus prone to generalize, it is not surprising that some of the exiles, Dante not least, were given to speculating on the Italian problem as such.

Dante's name has occurred twice in the last few pages. In mentioning him we are brought before another potent force in Italy as a whole: language and literature. It is true that the vernacular developed more slowly in Italy

[1] A. Pertile, *Storia del diritto italiano*, v (1892), 299–341.

than it did, for instance, in France; but it is also true that when it does emerge, in the late thirteenth century, it emerges in a singularly mature form. First and foremost here we must mention Dante's *De vulgari eloquentia*, for in it we have the first work by an Italian on the Italian problem as I have tried to outline it in previous pages: a dominant diversity, modified by certain cohesive pressures. His solution, the 'courtly Italian' which was to dog the *questione della lingua* for centuries, is in a sense less important than his realization that an Italian language was desirable, even necessary. And it is certainly less important than the way in which his own writings, and above all the *Divine Comedy*, became the model and master of later vernacular writing. It was not a rapid victory: because we can see the later dominance of Tuscan we must not assume that its triumph was either systematic or even assured; in a notable essay[1] Professor Dionisotti has reminded us that the very penetration of Tuscan in other areas is a subject hitherto inadequately studied. But after Dante there was, even if it was not viewed in this light, a *Florentine* classic; no other part of Italy had this and it was to make Tuscan invulnerable.

By the early fourteenth century, therefore, there were a number of characteristic features of Italian politics, society and culture which brought together the component parts of the country. The developments summarized in the term 'Renaissance' were, in my judgment, equally important as unifying influences. I hope to show this in subsequent chapters. In concluding this, however, I must

---

[1] C. Dionisotti, 'Geografia e storia della letteratura italiana', *Italian Studies*, VI (1951), 70–93; cf. Kristeller, *Studies in Renaissance Thought* (1956), p. 493.

emphasize once more the basic lack of political unity of Italy. To the outside world it might seem a homogeneous country—where Roman law was general, where men (even nobles and peasants) lived in towns and where slavery was a prominent feature of the social scene;[1] to the Italian himself there might be a wide range of attitudes, religious, social and economic, which he shared with most other Italians. 'As Italians we share some very simple habits of manners, customs and speech', is how we find it put in the *De vulgari eloquentia*.[2] But all of this was submerged in obtrusive differences, geographical and political and linguistic. To quote Dante again: '...curiam habemus, licet corporaliter sit dispersa': 'we have a single court, though it is physically scattered'.[3]

---

[1] For a brief but useful article on slavery, which is a subject important not only socially but also in much wider fields of art, literature and (perhaps) technological change, see Iris Origo, 'The domestic enemy: the eastern slaves in Tuscany in the fourteenth and fifteenth centuries', *Speculum*, XXX (1955), 321–66, and a good bibliography; cf. Lynn White, Jr., 'Tibet, India and Malaya as sources of western medieval technology', *Amer. Hist. Rev.*, LXV (1959–60), 515–26.

[2] I, xvi, 3.   [3] *De vulg. eloqu.* I, xviii, 5.

CHAPTER IV

POLITICS AND CULTURE
IN FOURTEENTH-CENTURY ITALY

For the first extended period in its history Italy in the fourteenth century was able to go her own way largely undisturbed by the conflict which had troubled her from the eleventh century between the claims of the Roman emperor of the west and those of the leader of the Western Christian church, the pope.[1] The emperors of the fourteenth century were, even when they could claim descent from an emperor, elective kings whose resources were those not of an empire but of their own German principality. Whatever Italians might feel about the emperor's overriding rights, about the basic legality he conferred on *de facto* authority,[2] the emperor was interested in Italy for only two reasons: to blackmail popes into crowning him; and to extract as much cash as possible from Italy in return for creating titles. His descents on Italy were now futile, not to say cynical, even when as elaborate

[1] The best manual is L. Simeoni (above, p. 43); Muratori's *Annali* and Sismondi's *Républiques* are still useful; so is the English version of Sismondi, in reality an independent book, by W. Boulting. P. Pieri, *Il Rinascimento e la crisi militare italiana*, Turin 1952, deals with far more than its title suggests and is especially valuable for the social structure of the different parts of Italy. Where not otherwise noted the political narrative in this and succeeding chapters will be found more fully discussed and vouched for in these works.

[2] F. Ercole, *Dal comune al principato*, Florence 1929, is a very stimulating book, which reprints, pp. 53–118, a celebrated essay on the emergence of Signori in the Veneto, and, pp. 119–354, the even more influential study of empire and papacy in Italian public law in the fourteenth and fifteenth centuries.

and as extended as Lewis of Bavaria's in 1327–30. They bulk largely in the text-books, for they offer to the Italian historian (and for much the same reason to the German) a line on which to peg his story, but they do not deserve this prominence.

In 1309 the city of Avignon welcomed the archbishop of Bordeaux, who had been elected pope as Clement V in 1305 after a stormy and protracted conclave. Clement's successors were to make Avignon their headquarters for the next seventy years. It would, of course, be wrong to think that the French popes of the fourteenth century were indifferent to Italy as a whole or to their particular territories, the States of the Church. Italy was probably their biggest single preoccupation: how to keep the emperor out of it; how to maintain order in, and secure the payment of dues from, their Italian lands; how to bolster up or restrain the power of the Angevins in Naples; how, in the end, to return to the city of Rome.[1] But an absentee pope was very differently placed from his predecessors who had never abandoned Italy for long, even if they had often not resided in Rome.

The fourteenth century gave a chance, therefore, for a less inhibited political development, and this might have been expected to have had cultural consequences as well. Before turning to these, however, we must examine the scene in a little greater detail. What was the country like which was more or less given its head? What were the main lines of its evolution? A short account of the position at the start of the century will do something to illustrate the

[1] G. Mollat, *Les papes d'Avignon*, 9th ed., Paris 1949, esp. pp. 137–308, with a copious bibliography.

argument of the preceding chapter that Italy was a very divided land.

In the north-west lay a number of territories loosely termed Savoy. Savoy proper straddled the Alps: one branch had its headquarters at Chambéry; another at Pinerolo. Round Saluzzo extended the county of that name and round Chivasso extended the power of the marquis of Montferrat. But these are simplifications, for feudal tenures gave scores of families and a few abbeys in all these areas virtual independence of the superior and considerable liberty of action. In addition there were a number of urban centres of importance, some under bishops and some under communal government: Ivrea, Turin, Vercelli, Alba, Asti, Alessandria, Cuneo and Mondovì. North of the Po in the central section of Northern Italy, each with fingers of land stretching up into the Alps, were Como, Novara, Milan (already under the Visconti), Bergamo, Brescia and Verona, with a fringe of communal states to the south of them: Pavia, Lodi, Crema, Cremona and Mantua. East of this the northernmost states, Feltre and Belluno, bordered on Austria, and so did Friuli: all of these territories, less urbanized than their neighbours, looked to their German lords and overlords, dukes of Austria and Carinthia, counts of Gorizia, as much as to the patriarch of Aquileia or the republic of Venice. Venice itself at the start of the fourteenth century had lands down the Dalmatian coast and in the east Mediterranean, but its share of the mainland consisted of two slices north and south of the Lagune, to which the territory of Padua came down; south of Padua lay the lands of Ferrara.

East of the Apennines and south of the Po, on the old Emilian road, a series of towns controlled bands of land: Piacenza, Parma, Reggio, Modena; but the hills still sheltered the extensive independent lands of the Malaspina and Pallavicini and even in the plain we should remember the lords of Correggio, Carpi and Mirandola. On the west of the central chain Genoese territory (which included the island of Corsica) lay along the coast almost reaching the confines of the Tuscan city of Lucca. Tuscany, besides Lucca, Pisa,[1] Florence and Siena, had a number of other considerable states—Volterra, Arezzo, S. Gimignano, Poggibonsi, Cortona; and also some extensive territories under feudal lords, of whom the greatest were the Aldobrandeschi.

Bordering Tuscany to the east of the Apennines and to the south were the States of the Church. Their northern limits were vague and depended on the obedience of Ferrara and Bologna. Internally towns and lordships jostled each other in an independence conditioned only by successful rivals and occasional papal activity: under Boniface VIII papal control was maintained by recognizing such independence, papal power was devoted to furthering the interests of the Caetani family—who with other great dynasties dominated the regions round Rome itself.

In the *regno* of Naples, one of the two 'Sicilies', strong government from the Normans onwards might have been expected to impose a uniformity and centralization lacking farther north. To some extent this had happened earlier. But by the early fourteenth century the crown, itself in

---

[1] Pisa in theory controlled Sardinia, but Boniface VIII had granted it to Aragon, and, after some resistance, Pisa accepted this in 1326.

theory dependent on the Roman pontiff, was itself merely the source of the privileges which enabled the unruly baronage to flout royal authority and some of the greater nobles to pursue entirely independent policies. A very large number of towns, a good many bishops, great abbeys (one of them, Benevento, dependent directly on the pope) added to the confusion. The territory was held together solely by the fisc, itself the cause of some of the most prolonged and damaging resistances to the king and his officers. Finally came the island which formed the southernmost part of Italy, the other 'Sicily' named officially 'Trinacria' by the peace of Caltabellotta (1302), under its Aragonese king. Here noble rivalries were exacerbated by hostility between the native aristocracy and the Catalans.

It follows from this picture of Italy that the factors which determined the actions of towns and great lords were for the most part local ambitions and fears. To understand the politics of even a large town like Florence one must descend to the particular. Certainly there were large combinations of powers: for and against the Della Scala, the Visconti. But these combinations, which play so large a part in the text-books, have often only transient importance and at most can only be understood in regional terms.[1] The most obvious illustration of this is the way in which Guelf and Ghibelline cease to have consistent meaning in four-teenth-century Italy: 'Ghibelline' Milan is found acting as papal watchdog; 'Guelf' Florence is at war with the Holy See. Note the extraordinary way in which King

---

[1] On regional groupings at this time, see the interesting article by G. Soranzo, 'Collegati, raccomandati, aderenti negli stati italiani dei secoli XIV e XV', *Archivio storico italiano*, XCIX (1941), I, 1–35.

Robert of Anjou acquired a kind of 'state' in North Italy, and a little later John of Bohemia; both were the product of the anxieties in small areas, seeking to preserve power locally by a nominal recognition of a seemingly powerful prince. Dante in welcoming Henry VII had no other purpose than to secure a kind of benevolent and lofty peacemaker who would have left untouched the 'liberty' of the Italian states. Yet some general observations may securely be made: the fourteenth century sees an unmistakable drift in North Italy from the free commune to the *signoria* of a man and his family; in Tuscany we have evidence that the free commune had greater success in resisting a similar trend; there was a gradual extension of a few states at what was ultimately to prove the permanent expense of others; and, with wide regional variations, the fourteenth century was a period of economic regression.

The emergence of the *signori* has been much discussed, and perhaps too much of a problem has been made of it. After all, most communes in Europe, and even in Italy, had a relatively short period of genuine independence; and some Italian towns never really left the control of the territorial lord. Granted the slender roots of the popular institutions on which communal independence rested, granted the acceptance everywhere of the notion of an ultimate superior, pope or emperor, it was not surprising that factions within a town should seize on the authority of an office to protect themselves against rivals. The magistrate thus exalted was still only *primus inter pares*; his jurisdiction rested on some kind of expression of popular approval; what had been done could be, and very often was, undone. In this sense the basis of power was and remained popular, at any rate for most of the fourteenth century, with the old assemblies surviving, responsible for a good deal of local law and administration and convoked regularly to sanction a change of ruler. Yet north and central Italy was the old 'Regnum Italiae' and the common law of the empire made it essential to secure legality by securing an imperial vicariate. This imperial vicariate was also, of course, granted to towns with republican forms of government. When it was conferred on a single lord it obviously bolstered up his power. But it did not create it. In Ercole's well-known definition, 'power came from below, from the people: sovereignty came from above, from the emperor'.[1] The same situation applied, *vis-à-vis* the pope, in the towns and lordships of the papal states.[2]

The Della Scala family represent a classic case of the process: the first Mastino emerged as leading citizen in Verona when the death of Ezzelin da Romano in 1259 released the city from a hated master. Soon Mastino became Captain of the People and not long after that acquired an imperial vicariate: a success that might have been personal was put on a more permanent footing by the ability of the brother and nephews who followed. Verona's lords arose in a city where the nobility had earlier been reduced to impotence. In Milan it was factions of nobles who provided rival leaders, the Della Torre for the merchant class, and the Visconti for the nobles. The victory went to the latter in 1278, under the guidance of the archbishop of Milan, Ottone Visconti, who before his death ensured the election of his nephew Matteo as Captain of the People; save for the reversal of 1302–10, the Visconti

[1] Ercole, *op. cit.* p. 271.   [2] *Ibid.* pp. 331 ff.

remained masters of the city until the middle of the fifteenth century. These two examples must suffice for the illustration of a process which is to be found in nearly every town of northern Italy: the queasy balance of parties within a town, the predominance of a family within a faction, a tradition of proscribing enemies and confiscating their property which envenomed even minor disputes, all contributed to the rapid extension of what contemporaries called tyranny.

The exceptions to this statement are none the less impressive: two Northern Italian towns escaped the fate of the rest, Venice and Genoa; and so, for long enough, did Bologna, if we may count it as a northern town. But the chief examples of viable republics are to be found in Tuscany. There are, of course, moments of wavering and moments even of capitulation: Florence put her lordship in the hands of Walter de Brienne, 'duke of Athens', for the disastrous year 1342–3; Lucca had the rule of Castruccio Castracani from 1316 to 1328; and Pisa gradually declined under the government, more or less concealed, of a series of families. Yet broadly speaking one may say that, however chaotic their internal history was, Florence, Lucca and Siena were genuine republics during the fourteenth century. The government in each was popular in that the nobles were excluded from power. It seems an inevitable conclusion that the mercantile cities of Tuscany, along with Genoa and Venice, maintained their communal constitution because of the strength that commerce and industry gave them, in contrast to the Lombard and Emilian towns.

Tyranny in Lombardy, communal government in

Tuscany had in common acquisitive policies that spelt the ruin and subjugation of other towns and tyrants. The empire of the Della Scala—from Verona they controlled by 1335 Vicenza, Treviso, Padua, Parma, Reggio, Lucca— was followed by the steadier but grander expansion of the Visconti. In a century they laid their hands on the whole of Lombardy, and when Giangaleazzo united the divided inheritance in his own hand (1385) the way was open to the south—to the States of the Church, to Tuscany. Less spectacular but no less important was the expansion of the republics. Venice admittedly drew back from advance on *terra firma* when her attempt to control Ferrara failed in 1308; she and Genoa had their hands full with maritime expansion and mutual rivalry. But Florence gradually extended her boundary to take in by the end of the fourteenth century nearly all of Tuscany save Lucca, Siena and Pisa. Some of these acquisitions by powerful governments can be attributed to economic pressures: a town was as strong as its contado; a contado was useless unless protected against attack; defence of trade routes and desire for the income from tolls both played a part. But already economics was giving way to politics, and when Giangaleazzo acquired a French princess as his wife and bought the title of duke from the emperor he was displaying the character of a new type of prince rather than that of the familiar tyrant; the dynamics of dynasticism was at work. Dynasticism was also effective in the north-west. There under Amadeus VI (d. 1383) the reintegration of the fiefs of Savoy was accomplished.

The fourth general observation is that the fourteenth century was, broadly speaking, a period of economic regression. In this Italy followed a trend common to Western Europe as a whole, though the varieties of economic activity in the peninsula made for infinite variation in the phasing of the decline and also for some notable exceptions. The drop in population and in agriculture and industrial production seems to have been particularly evident in Tuscany and especially at Florence. From the late thirteenth century we have bankruptcies on a significant scale; dearths of grain occur with monotonous frequency in the early fourteenth century, and the manufacture of cloth is seriously reduced. On top of this the Black Death of 1348 hit urban Italy and above all Tuscany with great violence: here as elsewhere its onset was heralded by widespread famine.[1] Nor was this economic decline of short duration. The recovery, partial and more readily to be seen in agriculture than in industry or commerce, was under way by the late fifteenth century but one may hazard the guess that even on the eve of the French invasion Italy was overall a less flourishing country than it had been in the middle of the thirteenth century.[2]

This, in broad terms, is the Italy in which the Renaissance was born. One of the notable characteristics of the Renaissance is that it corresponds in time to a period of acute strife in Italy, for the fourteenth century represents, I think it would be agreed, an epoch of conflict and confusion even

[1] See the references and figures in *IX congrès international des sciences historiques*, Paris 1950, I (*Rapports*), pp. 66–71 (by Cipolla, Dhondt, Postan, Wolff); *X congresso internazionale di scienze storiche*, Rome 1955, *Relazioni*, VI, 805–957 (by M. Mollat), esp. pp. 950–52; and, for Tuscany, the recent article by Enrico Fiumi, 'Fioritura e decadenza dell'economia fiorentina', pt. III, *Archivo storico italiano*, CXVII (1959), esp. pp. 472–86, 498–502 (this article deals in fact with other Tuscan towns as well as Florence).

[2] Cf. above, p. 3 and n.

by the standards of the divided Italy of the middle ages; likewise the Renaissance in Italy coincides with a time when the country was on the whole poorer than it had been. What were the stages in the development of the Renaissance? What influence did it have on the Italian scene in the fourteenth century?

The Renaissance comprised a new educational programme and a new attitude to literature and morality. It comprised a new art and a new place for art in the life of the individual and the community. How little of this we see in the fourteenth century! We are confronted then with individuals rather than with schools, with isolated monuments rather than with an accepted style. It is the age of Petrarch and Boccaccio, of Giotto.

The future was to lie with a revived interest in the classics, yet we must be careful not to assume an unbroken progress from the 'pre-humanists', French or North Italian, of the twelfth and thirteenth centuries, through the masters of the fourteenth century, down to the triumph of the new ways in the fifteenth.[1] It is not the least curious feature of Renaissance studies that Italian developments of the fourteenth century are relatively ill-documented. We must echo the observation of Professor Roberto Weiss: only when further work has been devoted

---

[1] The only systematic account of the literary renaissance remains Georg Voigt, *Die Wiederbelebung des classischen Alterthums*, Berlin 1859; 2nd ed., 2 vols., Berlin 1880–1; 3rd ed., 2 vols., Berlin 1893 (edited by Max Lehnerdt). The second German edition was translated into Italian by D. Valbusa, 2 vols., Florence 1888, with additional notes, some of which were not incorporated by Lehnerdt. Books I and II were translated into French, from the 3rd German edition, by A. le Monnier (Paris 1894), with a few relatively unimportant additions. References in what follows are to the third German edition.

to the scholars of early fourteenth-century Florence, Bologna, Verona and Naples, only when a general study of literature at Padua has been undertaken, shall we be able to generalize with security on the humanities before Petrarch.[1] Yet, as the same authority has pointed out else-where,[2] the striking thing about the coteries of learned men who took an interest in cultivating the literature of ancient Rome was that they were predominantly lawyers. And in pointing to their connections with earlier move-ments in France and to the Roman law which encouraged them to regard antiquity as a fountain of living example, he has surely put his finger on matters of significance.

On an earlier page I ventured to say that the two most important bequests of the Latin world to medieval Italy were urban civilization and the Roman law. The two go together, of course, but the second pursued its own independent way in determining intellectual interests in medieval Italy. These interests are in sharp contrast with Northern Europe. There are no great cathedral schools south of the Alps. The Italian university developed faculties of theology tardily and they were never influential. Is it an accident that the great Italian scholastics, Anselm, Peter Lombard, Bonaventura, Aquinas, flowered (so to speak) in French soil? The specifically Italian contribution to medieval civilization must be sought for in the works of Joachim of Flora, St Francis and the author of the Golden Legend, Jacopo da Voragine, and above all in the lawyers. The nearest thing to the Sorbonne in Italy was Bologna.

---

[1] R. Weiss, *Il primo secolo dell'umanesimo*, Rome 1949, p. 10.
[2] R. Weiss, *The Dawn of Humanism in Italy*, London 1947; this inaugural lecture is the best survey of the subject.

From Irnerius in the eleventh century and Gratian in the twelfth, the finest intellectual talent in Italy gravitated to civil and canon law. The chain of canonists, of glossators and post-glossators is long and unbroken. The legist, from the humble notary upwards, was assured of subsistence, and sometimes obtained great wealth and public esteem. The civilian staffed the administrative departments of towns and princes; the canonist could rise to be pope.

The profession of the law must thus be considered seriously in any discussion of cultural developments in Italy, for it had an important bearing on what made Italy very different from the North. It meant among other things that facilities for the education of lawyers were widely diffused in Italy, and by no means restricted to university towns. Florence, for example, which had no university, had a notarial school of which she was most proud.[1] It meant that the main bent of Italian learning was towards the concrete, the practical problems of government and administration, rather than towards the metaphysical or the theological. It meant that at universities teaching was directed to older students and that it had in mind a forensic purpose which linked grammar and rhetoric to practical applications. And it meant that the bulk of these students were not even technically (as clerks were in the North) clergy.[2] The stress on law encouraged, if it did not spring from, a secular strain in the intellectual life of the peninsula; it was directed to practical questions and the cut and thrust of the courts; and, as we have noted, it took

[1] Dati wrote in his *Istoria di Firenze* 'la fonte de' dottori delle leggi è Bologna, e la fonte de' dottori della notaria è Firenze'; Voigt, I, 392, n. 1.

[2] Cf. H. Rashdall, *Universities of Europe in the Middle Ages*, ed. Powicke and Emden, 3 vols., Oxford 1936, I, 91 and n.

men back not to the Bible but to the *Codex* and the *Digest*, to classical antiquity as the source of at any rate one kind of truth.

When one examines the production of the lawyer-littérateurs of the late thirteenth and early fourteenth centuries one is, however, bound to be disappointed. Much, it is true, has not survived. Is that not a pointer to the quality of some of this activity? Of what has survived one is struck by its superficial quality. I do not mean only that their verses are often a tissue of phrases lifted from favourite classical authors, though this seems often to be the case.[1] I mean that, despite their legal training, despite the practical twist of their legal background, these men are not much concerned with practical problems, with the moral issues which were to obtrude so strikingly in the work of their successors. They were certainly concerned with some important literary questions: Lovato dei Lovati, the Paduan judge who died in 1309, explained the metres of Seneca's tragedies; Giovanni de Matociis, a clergyman and not a lawyer, who was a contemporary at Verona of Lovati, distinguished for the first time between the two Plinies.[2] And their lack of concern with political and moral questions must not be pressed too far. If Geri d'Arezzo (d. before 1339), whom Salutati was to record as one of the two notable precursors of Petrarch, displayed a conventional distaste for women and marriage in one of his few surviving letters,[3] both he and Lovati

[1] See, for example, the analysis by Guido Billanovich, '"Veterum vestigia vatum" nei carmi dei preumanisti padovani', *Italia medioevale e umanistica*, I (1958), 155–243.

[2] See Weiss, *Dawn*, pp. 6–7, 13–14.

[3] Weiss, *Primo secolo*, pp. 112–14.

wrote pieces on the Guelf–Ghibelline strife which have not survived and which might have shown a more original political awareness.[1] More important, much less amateurish in all respects than the rest, is Albertino Mussato (1261–1329).

Mussato is a more prominent person than any of the other writers who were touched by the new appeal of antiquity. His career in many ways anticipates the future: he was an unwilling schoolmaster in his early days; he turned to the law and public service; as ambassador and soldier he defended the interests of his city, and in 1315 he was crowned, the first laureation of a poet.[2] He wrote history in a manner more influenced by antique models than earlier Italians. He composed in his play *Ecerinis* not merely the first Senecan tragedy, but a work in which knowledge of, and sympathy for, antiquity are devoted to the service of the state: the drama of the career of Ezzelin was a parable designed to encourage Padua to resist the ambitions of Can Grande della Scala. All of this, clumsy though it is, is in the grand manner: it reminds one of Petrarch, Salutati, Bruni; one wonders what his missing autobiography would have been like.[3]

---

[1] Weiss, *Dawn*, p. 6; *Primo secolo*, pp. 60–1.

[2] A recent study of laureation is worth noting: J. B. Trapp, 'The Owl's Ivy and the Poet's Bays', *Journ. Warb. and Court. Inst.* XXI (1958), 227–55.

[3] The broad view of Paduan liberty and of a tyranny threatening Italy may be seen in these lines:

> ECERINUS: Capiamus urbes undique et late loca.
> Verona Vicentia Padua nutu meo
> Iam subiacent: progrediar ulterius cito.
> Promissa Lombardia me dominum vocat:
> Habere puto. Meos nec ibi sistam gradus.
> Italia michi debetur.
>
> (*Ecerinide*, ed. Luigi Padrin, Bologna 1900, p. 41.)

The emergence of these scholars in the early decades of the fourteenth century poses certain questions. So much of their activity resembles early French activities—where Latin verse was cultivated, commentaries composed on ancient authors, texts of whom were assiduously assembled —that it has sometimes been asserted that at Padua and elsewhere we are seeing French influence at work.[1] But these remain assertions, without any proof. More important, there has been a marked tendency to treat the Latin exercises quite separately from developments in the vernacular. It is surely significant that the new interest in the writings of antiquity coincided with the emergence of vernacular literature. Are we in short not seeing in the Italy of Dante's day a general cultural revival, not dissimilar from earlier French developments, but *sui generis*, marked by all those characteristically Italian features we have earlier had occasion to remark? Professor Kristeller has rightly pointed to the continuity of the literary tradition, closely associated with law and medicine, which links fourteenth-century Italian scholarship with earlier Italian practices: 'I do not hesitate to conclude that the eloquence of the humanists was the continuation of the medieval *ars aregandi* iust as their epistolography continued the tradition of the *ars dictaminis*.'[2] Finally let us not too readily jump to the conclusion that with Lovati, Mussato and the rest the new literary attitudes were either fully expressed or generally revived. In many ways the early fourteenth-century movement is a dead end: the Padua of Mussato does not respond

[1] B. L. Ullman, 'Some Aspects of the Origin of Italian Humanism', *Philological Quarterly*, xx (1941), 212–23; Kristeller, *Studies*, pp. 570–1.

[2] *Studies*, p. 566. See below, p. 121 n. 3 for Salutati's recognition as a master of 'rhetoric and *ars dictaminis*'.

to his classical patriotism as the Florence of Salutati and Bruni was to accept their contributions; Padua falls to the Carrara family as agents of the Della Scala in 1328 and Mussato dies in exile.

It does not seem to me to be fanciful to link with these innovations artistic developments which are roughly contemporary. Nicola Pisano, we are told, embodied in his reliefs that new French way of depicting reality which in its turn was inspired in all probability by antique models. Then Giotto turned this achievement in sculpture, always a more sophisticated art form than painting, into two-dimensional representation. Why Nicola Pisano, with Roman sarcophagi around him in the Camposanto at Pisa, should need French influence to make his innovations seems to me far from clear. And in Giotto's case French influence has to be supplemented by Byzantine in order to explain his astonishing originality. Leaving aside the question of the artistic ancestry of Nicola Pisano and Giotto, however, let us note that here too we find a check. The inventions of the early fourteenth century are not immediately exploited: it was, indeed, and somewhat paradoxically, a wave of northern influence which in the mid-fourteenth century subjugated Italian art and architecture. As in literature, one might say, so in art early fourteenth-century Italy was not quite ready for a fresh style.

It has been remarked that the three great figures of fourteenth-century Italian cultural history, Dante, Petrarch and Boccaccio, were singularly rootless, their careers exceptional, their works somewhat exotic.[1] Of none is

[1] Cf. Dionisotti, 'Geografia e storia', p. 81.

this truer than Francesco Petrarca, the greatest single figure in the story I am trying to tell.[1] If Dante sums up the past, Petrarch provides a programme for the future and we know a great deal about it through the exuberant material he provided about himself, his aims and his accomplishments. Nothing is more remarkable than the bulk of Petrarch's letters, and his attitude towards this kind of writing, this living through a pen; and if anything could be more remarkable it is his *Secret*, the book in which he debates with Augustine over his ambitions, the first document to be discussed in that unwritten history of European intro-spection.

For those who wish to trace a kind of apostolic tradition in the reawakening humanities Petrarch is an awkward case.[2] The specific genius of Italy lay, as we have seen, in the essentially secular subjects of law and medicine, while in France a similar predominance is found in theology and metaphysics. On both establishments Petrarch, who was a clerk and not a layman, deliberately turned his back. This son of a Tuscan exile at Avignon was put to the law by his father and retained from his experience of it a lasting loathing of the *legulei*; his contempt for medical men was equally thorough. As for the teaching of the schools of France his condemnation was no less severe: the famous

---

[1] Voigt, I, 21–156; P. de Nolhac, *Pétrarque et l'humanisme*, 2nd ed., 2 vols., Paris 1907, remains the basic study; J. H. Whitfield, *Petrarch and the Renascence*, Oxford 1943, is an extremely perceptive study of the Latin works. For the Italian poetry see N. Sapegno, *Il Trecento*, with full bibliography, Milan 1934; and E. H. Wilkins, *The Making of the 'Canzoniere' and other Petrarchan Studies*, Rome 1951.

[2] It can be done, however, by stressing Petrarch's attendance at the University of Bologna, 1320–6, where in 1319 Giovanni del Vergilio had been appointed to lecture on the Latin poets.

invective called 'On his own ignorance and that of other people' has been the subject of a good deal of recent work from which it emerges that Padua at that time cannot be held responsible for the Averroists attacked by the poet;[1] but the burden of his argument remains, that 'the crazy and clamorous set of Scholastics' had practically deified Aristotle, that the commentary—the basis of philosophical exposition—was too often an occasion for servile adherence to received opinion, that dialectic was too often made an end in itself.[2] Petrarch wrote this invective when he was sixty-three, and famous. One may suspect that what hurt him in the criticisms of the four Venetian friends was less their espousal of Aristotle and Averroes than their denial of his literary ability and social standing. Why was Petrarch famous in his own day?

This may sound a rhetorical question, but it is not. In 1341, when the poet at the age of thirty-six was crowned on the Capitol, in the tradition of Mussato and of Dante's dead body, his literary output was negligible so far as Latin was concerned, and we may take it that his fame as a vernacular poet was obviously present in the minds of his sponsors, even if it was for his Latin writings that he was

[1] P. O. Kristeller, 'Petrarch's Averroists', *Bib. d'humanisme et renaissance*, XIV (1952), 59–65; Kristeller in *La civiltà veneziana del trecento*, Florence 1956, pp. 149–78; B. Nardi in *La civiltà veneziana del quattrocento*, Florence 1957, pp. 101–45. It was Renan who antedated the moment (1405) when Padua might legitimately be called a Venetian 'quartier latin'. Much stress is laid on the *De sui ipsius et multorum ignorantia* in the thesis of G. Toffanin, that the main current of Renaissance thought was specifically directed against the 'scientific' attitude of the schools; see for instance his *Storia dell'umanesimo dal XIII al XV secolo*, 3rd ed., Bologna 1947, pp. 83–137.

[2] *De sui ipsius et multorum ignorantia*, ed. L. M. Capelli, Paris 1906, pp. 72–4 *et passim*; a useful translation, with notes, of the whole work and related passages from other writings by H. Nachod in *The Renaissance Philosophy of Man*, ed. E. Cassirer, P. O. Kristeller, J. H. Randal, Jr., Chicago 1948, pp. 47–143.

given the crown of immortality. As far as the Latin works are concerned it has been truly said: 'the invitations to be crowned were extended on the basis of faith rather than of performance'[1]—invitations because there were two, one from Paris and another, which Petrarch accepted, from Rome. The explanation is that Petrarch cleverly, and (as subsequently was to be proved) justifiably, persuaded certain influential men of his own value as poet and historian, the names by which he was qualified in the coronation. He was, that is to say, aiming at fame, a point which contrasts with Dante's ironical reply to Giovanni del Vergilio who suggested that Dante could be crowned at Bologna, if only he would abandon the unworthy vernacular and write a poem in Latin.[2] Dante, like Petrarch, was celebrated as a poet in Italian: unlike Petrarch, Dante was not prepared to deny Italian for the kind of academic accolade which laureation was.

We are brought thus face to face with the earliest of Petrarch's dilemmas: his vernacular verses and his consciousness of the superior nobility of Latin. He regularly referred to his sonnets, *Triumphs* and other vernacular poetry as *juvenilia*.[3] But the facts challenge this: he still from time to time wrote Italian verse and in the last ten years of his life he was still arranging the *Canzoniere*.[4] The Italian poems are thus as long-lived a preoccupation as the Latin writings, though they ceded pride of place, at any rate officially, to the Latin epic *Africa*, the letters and the treatises. So that at any rate part of the reason for Petrarch's

[1] Wilkins, *op. cit.* p. 35; cf. the table on p. 30.
[2] Cf. Wilkins, pp. 23–4; Trapp, *art. cit.* p. 238.
[3] Wilkins, p. 291.
[4] *Ibid.* pp. 287–93.

contemporary reputation was his Italian poetry—a reputation he encouraged to the end of his life and which, as things have turned out, has been the side of his genius most acceptable to later ages.

Against the steady appreciation accorded to the Italian poems we must set the ups and downs in his reputation as a moralist in Latin, though we need not follow these to their present position, where Petrarch's admirers have perhaps overstated their significance. What is important in Petrarch's prose from the viewpoint of his contemporaries is undoubtedly his new insistence on the moral value of literature, and the basic part in that to be played by the literature of antiquity. Literature was the means of self-improvement, of improvement in society; literature, in a word, was life. The works in which Petrarch demonstrated his thesis were not all of startling originality: his views on many questions were traditional and confused; a pleasant and very human inconsistency indeed facilitated the reception of his method. He could argue at one moment the stultifying effect of formal religion, at another praise the monk. Love is ethereal and good, or carnal and bad: Laura who inspired his lyrical poetry, and the mistress or mistresses by whom he had his children. He is a clergyman and bitter critic of the Babylonish captivity; he is greedy for more benefices and is the very type of non-resident. All of this and more we can see in his letters, his dialogues and essays, all of it expressed with a fluency and freeness which swept off their feet some of the clerks with their stuffy letterbooks and a few of the rulers with their stuffy clerks. What Petrarch did in his Latin books and letters was to reflect the living world around him in an entirely novel way.

This demonstration of the virtuosity of Latin as a vehicle of reality was, of course, more than just a personal triumph of a gifted writer. No other language could at that time have carried the kind of writing which Petrarch was producing: the vernaculars were capable of superb verse, as Dante had shown, as Petrarch himself showed. But verse makes fewer demands of a language than prose: it is less complicated in the resources it requires; and in Italy as elsewhere there was no one accepted literary vernacular, as we have seen. As for the Latin of the schools, of the monk, of the administrator, it had become a cumbersome and clumsy medium—corrupted by the dialects around it, a language which was in practice one of convenience and not of art. From this Babel Petrarch turned to the language of Cicero and Virgil to reveal its strength and subtlety, its possibilities of perfection, its ability to carry moods, nuances of sentiment, the epigram. Its use was another dimension. And with this joy in literature we move into a new world, where one no longer need relegate *trivia* to a despised vernacular and reserve for a solemn Latinity all that is serious and sober: one has one language doing the whole job—the model at which vernaculars were later to aim. This programme was not fulfilled by Petrarch: like Dante before him and like his contemporary Boccaccio, Petrarch had a kind of linguistic ambivalence: all three in practice wrote most of their verse in Italian, their treatises in Latin. But Petrarch marked the way with his epic *Africa* which, even if unsuccessful, was a portent of future trends, especially in the *Volgare*. One other gesture by Petrarch may be mentioned here—his adoption of a different script. To us, accustomed as we are to the finished

products of Roman and Italic hands which have deter
mined the style in which we all write and in which all ou
books are printed, his efforts may seem primitive. The
were, however, the start of a revolution in writing which
as developed by the next generation of Florentines and
adopted by the printer, was to have profound educationa
and aesthetic consequences.[1]

These remarks may suggest that Petrarch's fame was du
solely to his manner, that *what* he said is less importan
than *how* he said it. This is not true, though I suspect recen
scholarship has unduly neglected the artist in Petrarch.
In particular we must recognize one basic position which
commanded contemporary respect and later emulation
and note two particular applications of it.[3] The basi
position is that Petrarch found in much of the writing o
classical authors, and notably in Cicero and (if we ma
allow him as a classic) Augustine, a guidance more appro
priate to the problems of his life than he found in the
traditional teaching of the West: they, too, not only wrot
well, but they thought well. From this flowed Petrarch'
docta pietas, his reverence for *philosophia*, his desire to under
stand himself as a social animal and as an intellectual anima
and as a literary animal. To quote the fine phrase o
Professor Whitfield, Petrarch's work 'lies in the firm re-

[1] Since these pages were written B. L. Ullman's *The Origin and Developmen
of Humanistic Script* has appeared, Rome 1960. In this the argument is pu
forward that Poggio was responsible for the script which was ultimately to b
described, in its printed form, as 'Roman', and Niccolò Niccoli for the hand
which was to be known as 'italic'.

[2] I mean in *all* his writing, not in the Italian poems where his merit ha
never been neglected.

[3] For the rest of this chapter and for much of the rest of the book I hav
found much help in E. Garin, *L'umanesimo italiano*, Bari 1952.

establishment of a study which had been neglected for centuries...which is, of course, not so much antiquity as moral philosophy with the guidance of antiquity'.[1] Education, in short, was seen not as the training of clerics, or even ledger-keepers: but of the whole man. Its purpose was the old purpose, to please God, but by 'planning human life so that it may be fair and pleasing' in His sight.[2]

The two particular applications of this recovered insistence on the relevance of moral philosophy which must be examined are the question of the active life and the problem of Italy. Consideration of the second of these I want to postpone for a moment.[3]

The starkest possible contrast between the ancients and the moderns—the fourteenth-century moderns—lay in the priority accorded by Christian teaching to renunciation. 'Love not the things that are in the world'; 'my kingdom is not of this world'; 'the wisdom of this world is foolishness with God'; 'flesh and blood cannot inherit the kingdom of God'.[4] These are the texts that hung above the Christian as he made his way about created nature: they are unequivocal. They took men to the desert, they peopled the monasteries, they recruited for the friars. They lay like a load on the baron and the peasant, the merchant and the soldier—and on many a priest and monk. They even led to a view of Greek philosophy and of Roman thought compatible with this. The Aristotle of the middle ages, like the Cicero of the middle ages, was a recluse. In so far as they

---

[1] J. H. Whitfield, *Petrarch and the Renascence*, Oxford 1943, p. 47.
[2] *Ibid.* p. 71.
[3] Below, p. 93.
[4] I John ii. 15; John xviii. 36; I Corin. iii. 19, xv. 50.

were masters they joined the company of hermits. Some of this strange adaptation was modified in the thirteenth century, when Aristotle became a schoolman and Cicero's *De officiis* was studied at Paris; but it was Petrarch who was the first really to recognize the anguish of the problem.[1]

As Dr Baron has shown, it was Petrarch's discovery of the letters to Atticus which revealed Cicero in a new light. This was in 1345. But for a realization of the full influence of this discovery we should, I feel, consider, as Dr Baron had no space to do in his masterly, indeed epoch-making essay, how the discovery coincided with a particular moment of Petrarch's life. The *peregrinus ubique*, as Petrarch called himself,[2] had spent nearly the whole of his forty-odd years in travel, with only short periods of permanent residence: he had moved about a great deal in France and Italy and knew each country from north to south. On the other hand from 1337 he had spent a few years based on Vaucluse, his rustic retreat near Avignon. Already, that is to say, he had experienced to the full both the involvement and incident of the active life and (though more briefly) the rewards of withdrawal from it. More important still the dilemma of withdrawal or commitment had been dramatized by him in his finest work, the *Secretum* which was written in 1342–3 during a second period of residence at Vaucluse. This remarkable work is a dialogue between Augustine and Petrarch in which

[1] Hans Baron, 'Cicero and the Roman Civic Spirit in the Middle Ages and the Early Renaissance', *Bull. J. Rylands Library*, XXII (1938), 1–28; Garin, *op. cit.* pp. 27–50.

[2] See the most useful chapter so entitled, with its list of Petrarch's change of residence, in Wilkins, *op. cit.* pp. 1–8.

[3] *Opera omnia*, Basle 1581, pp. 331–69; translated W. H. Draper, London 1911.

the saint propounds the only road to virtue—to break the fetters of the world by perpetual meditation on death— and Petrarch, while conceding this, postpones the abandonment of his previous life which should follow. The analysis of Petrarch's predicament is taken from life itself: 'de medio experientiae libro';[1] his career, his loves, his *accidia* or *aegritudo* are all dispassionately examined. And he accepts as right, even if his present preoccupations prevent him from embodying the truth of it in his life, the doctrine that 'a wise man's life is all one preparation for death: *tota philosophorum vita commentatio mortis est*'. The phrase is taken by Petrarch from Cicero, as Cicero had taken it from Plato.[2] Under the guidance of Augustine and Cicero, Petrarch accepts the theory of the vanity of human activities.

The letters to Atticus present a different Cicero from the sage who wrote on death and on friendship. They reveal a Cicero who used the eloquence so greatly admired by Petrarch not for the inculcation of virtue or the criticism of folly and pedantry. They show 'a Roman citizen, who had given up his offices in the state under compulsion, in consequence of Caesar's victory; a citizen who, from his rural retreat, followed political events feverishly, and who, after the murder of Caesar, returned to the confusion of civil war, to his own ruin'.[3] When we remember the part of counsellor which Cicero plays in the *Secretum* to both Augustine and Petrarch we can understand the short, bitter letter the latter addressed to the shade of Cicero, 'from the land of

[1] *Opera omnia*, p. 358; Draper, p. 137.
[2] *Opera omnia*, p. 368; Draper, p. 189; Cic., *Tusc.* I, 30, 74; the text in Petrarch runs: 'tota philosophorum commendatio mortis est'.
[3] Baron, 'Cicero', pp. 16–17.

the living...in Verona on 16 June in the year 1345 of that Lord whom you never knew': 'O ever breathlessly unquiet, or—in your own words—rash and unhappy old man, why could you not detach yourself from so much worthless strife? Why did you throw away the calm which best suited your age, your rank and your future? What deceptive glory bewitched you...and in the end brought you to a death shameful in a wise' man?'[1] And so on. We can also see why the hermit of Vaucluse and Arquà later argued that the philosophical works of Cicero were the fruit of retirement, even if involuntary; despite himself he is an example of the virtue of *otium*, a warning of the hazards of *negotium*.[2] We shall see in the sequel that this question was to be further debated, by men prepared to face the lesson of Cicero more boldly than Petrarch.

The passionate identification of the *studia humanitatis* with life, the new interests which could be stimulated and satisfied through a sympathetic concern with antiquity, these were Petrarch's bequests to his contemporaries—bequests which have a richness not found in the earlier cultivators of antiquity in France or Italy. But it is not the case that the cultivation of the humanities followed at once as a result of Petrarch's example. Petrarch was no teacher and what was needed was formal instruction. He was, and tried to be, above the factions and loyalties of his native land. It was essential that the importance he attached to the humanities should become rooted in localities where it could grow and develop.

In some ways the moment was propitious. The groups

---

[1] *Ep. Fam.* XXIV, 3.　　　[2] Baron, 'Cicero', p. 17.

of scholars and men of affairs found in so many Italian towns were responsive to the stimulus of Petrarch's writings—collections of which were soon formed by others than the author himself. The legal and medical traditions of the university in Italy had encouraged secular education in the arts and mercantile interests provided relatively numerous schools where the sons of merchants could learn to calculate.[1] Among the throng of teachers, among whom the 'free', i.e. non-clerical, soon had the predominance, there were those who delighted in literature in a fresh way.

The movement of educational change in fourteenth-century Italy is, however, a slow process, it would seem.[2] The masters interested in and responsive to Petrarch are scattered and lack a formal programme. There is Convenevole da Prato, Petrarch's own teacher, who was brought back to his home town and honoured on his death with laureation in 1338. There is Giovanni del Vergilio, who was given a chair at Bologna in 1319. At Florence we find Bruno Casini (d. 1348) and Zanobi da Strada, who was laureated at Pisa in 1355; at Verona Gasparo Squaro de Broaspini, Petrarch's copyist; and there are others besides, who have left memorials of their interest in the humanities or who figure as correspondents of Petrarch.[3]

---

[1] G. Manacorda, *Storia della scuola in Italia*, 1. *Il medio evo*, 2 vols., Milan n.d. [1914], and especially the topographical lists (*Dizionario geografico*) in II, 283–337.

[2] Studies of humanist education deal almost exclusively with the theorists of the fifteenth century: a general study of the grammar school in the previous century would be very useful; failing that there is much scattered information in Manacorda.

[3] Cf. Sapegno, *Trecento* (Milan 1934), p. 159: Rinaldo Cavalchini; Moggio de' Moggi; Donato Albanzani da Pratovecchio; Anastasio d'Ubaldo Gezzi da Ravenna; Pietro da Muglio.

The list is not particularly impressive, but we must bear in mind the troubled state of Italy which reacted on her universities, reducing their numbers and their influence,[1] and we must also remember that what Petrarch propounded and exemplified was a different attitude to letters, not in itself a new curriculum. Certainly Petrarch was concerned to find new texts of classical authors and better texts of those he knew. But it has often been pointed out that the basic classics of Petrarch were those well enough known through the middle ages—the pabulum of the schools, the substance of the teaching of the *grammaticus*. Wherever there was a grammarian we can find some Cicero, Virgil, Ovid. For example at Chioggia, not a famous centre, the pupils of the local school were divided, as commonly in Italy, into 'latinantes' and 'non-latinantes'. Those 'qui sunt de Latino' are described as 'volentes audire tragedias, Vergilium, Lucanum, Terentium, et similes poetas'.[2] Granted the existence of a new approach, the old teaching could yield a fresh harvest. When we meet, at the end of the fifteenth century, two or three great schoolmasters, themselves the teachers of generations of humanists, we need not feel that we must account for their existence. As Petrarch had acquired his learning from Convenevole da Prato and the schools of Bologna but put it to new use, so with Giovanni Malpaghini and Giovanni di Conversino.[3]

Only in one field was it necessary to make special provision: Greek was, despite the provisions of the Council

---

[1] S. D'Irsay, *Histoire des universités*, 2 vols., Paris 1933–5, I, 236; Rashdall, *Universities*, II, 1–62, covers Italian universities other than Salerno and Bologna, which are dealt with in vol. I.

[2] Manacorda, I, 180–1.

[3] Below, pp. 136, 154.

of Vienne, in 1312,[1] not taught in Western universities and *a fortiori* had no place in secondary education. Petrarch's enthusiasm for the literature which Cicero admired is well known. So are his fruitless efforts to learn the language. Theoretically this should have been easy in Italy, for large areas in the south retained the language from the time of Magna Graecia: it is indeed still a patois in a few places in Calabria.[2] Old-fashioned and unoriginal though they were, the Basilian monks occasionally produced scholars; so did the Greek secular clergy. Yet it has been authoritatively stated that they had no real place in Renaissance Greek studies:[3] few were adequately bilingual, and on top of that they were tinged with heresy, tended to look to Constantinople for intellectual leadership and were regarded suspiciously by the Roman hierarchy. The result was that Western scholars turned to Byzantium itself for help, as Petrarch looked to Barlaam of Seminara who, though Calabrian born, came to Petrarch's notice while on a visit to the curia at Avignon after many years' residence at Constantinople. Teaching an adult Petrarch who knew more than his master about all that was classical in Greek save the tongue itself cannot have been easy and Barlaam did not succeed. Petrarch's ambition to read Homer was then, it will be remembered, to be satisfied

---

[1] That Paris, Bologna, Oxford, Salamanca and the Curial University should appoint professors of Greek, Arabic, Chaldee and Hebrew. Nothing much seems to have come of this, though some action seems to have been taken at the Curial University and at Oxford: Rashdall, II, 30–1; III, 161–2.

[2] On Greek in fourteenth-century Italy see R. Weiss, 'The Greek Culture of South Italy in the Later Middle Ages', *Proc. Brit. Acad.* XXXVII (1951), 23–50; Kenneth M. Setton, 'The Byzantine Background to the Italian Renaissance', *Proc. Amer. Phil. Soc.* C (1956), 1–76.

[3] Weiss, 'Greek Culture', p. 45.

by a translation commissioned of Leontius Pilatus, a Calabrian whom Boccaccio discovered. The career of the wretched man, boorish, unpleasant and not a scholar, is of little interest beyond the establishment for him of a chair of Greek at Florence in 1360. This major effort came to a rapid end; the Greek left in 1363 and died in 1365 or 1366; in any case he attracted to his lectures only Boccaccio and a few others. A still more significant indication of the slow educational response of Italy to Petrarch's insistence on the importance of Greek is provided by the career of Simon Atumano, a Greek of unquestioned scholarly competence, who had been promoted by Urban V to the archbishopric of Thebes: when he was teaching at Rome in 1380–1 he apparently had only one pupil.[1]

It was stated above that for the *studia humanitatis*, the liberal disciplines, to flourish they had to strike roots. Petrarch, voluntary exile from his native Tuscany, moved round the princely courts of Italy, flirted with the Venetian Republic, but did not respond to invitations to settle in Florence. Yet at no other town was his teaching to penetrate more deeply or more quickly. For this there are many reasons, doubtless, but three strike one as particularly compelling: the nature of Florentine society, the character of Petrarch's vernacular writings, and the efforts of Giovanni Boccaccio.

Mid-fourteenth-century Florence is in many ways similar to other Italian towns which had succeeded in averting the rule of a single *signore*. A dominant class of rich merchants, having excluded from power the nobility,

[1] Setton, *op. cit.* pp. 49–50.

governed the city with the smaller merchants and wealthier craftsmen as junior partners, and the lower orders entirely excluded from participation in government. The government of the *Grassi* was faction-ridden; the nobles nursed their resentment; the ambitions of the unprivileged was slowly becoming vocal. What made Florence different from Pisa, Lucca, Siena and other Tuscan republics, as well as from Genoa and Venice, was her great wealth and her industrial development. The combination of banking with the manufacture and processing of cloth, especially woollens, had made a large number of Florentines rich, and had turned an even larger number into proletarians. No other town in Italy could produce this particular social mixture, for at Venice, where comparable, perhaps greater, wealth was to be found, an entirely different economic development had precluded the development of large-scale manufacturing industry, while socially the Venetian merchant became 'noble'[1]. The Florentine banker ventured his money all over the Christendom where he also traded; the economy of the city turned on the economy of Europe. Alert, canny, immensely literate in the language of trade, the Florentine merchant was also suspicious in public affairs; the ruling group devised machinery which was designed to avoid the possession of power by a few clans, let alone an individual. Short-term magistracies, a mixture of lot and ballot, meant a perpetual public interest in politics, a perpetual concern for the preservation of what Florentines called 'liberty', and, of course, a perpetual state of factions, intrigue and uncertainty. It also meant an

---

[1] On the different economic and social development of Italian towns see Y. Renouard, *Les Hommes d'affaires italiens au moyen âge*, Paris 1949.

awareness perhaps sharper than elsewhere of the contrasts between the teachings of the church and the realities of daily life, or, to use the new phraseology, between *otium* and *negotium*. The merchant's account-books, with their invocation of the Mosaic commandments and their percentage to 'Domeneddio' (God) were a reminder that it was not easy for a rich man to enter the kingdom of heaven; and so were the churches, above all the cathedral, so light without, so gaunt and grim within [Plate XII], no more than a huge hall for the sermon which played a great part in the life of the Florentine.

Petrarch was born at Arezzo, a town occupied by Florence from 1336 to 1343 and intimately involved in Florentine policy thereafter until it was reacquired in 1384; Petrarch's father was a Florentine merchant; Petrarch's Italian poetry was written in Tuscan. These were grounds enough for Florentine interest in Petrarch, even if during his lifetime the profounder implications of his Latin works, with their awareness of the place of the here-below as against traditional denial of it, made little headway. His poetry was immediately accessible to a people whose interest in literature at every level was remarkable. The cultivation of artistic verse and prose in Tuscany and above all in the upper and middle ranks of Florentine society made enormous strides in the fourteenth century. At the other end of the social scale the production of irreverent and acrimonious verse delighted the Florentine groundlings —who were also capable of digesting more exalted verse if the stories in Sacchetti about Dante have any basis in reality.[1] The refined verse of Petrarch was immediately at

[1] Sacchetti, *Trecento novelle*, nos. CXIV, CXV, pp. 254–7.

home in the cultivated circles of Florence and soon had an even wider public there.

The efforts of Giovanni Boccaccio to establish the new attitude to literature and learning in his native city were thus backed by a popular culture extensive in the vernacular, and by probably as much, if not more, Latin grammar schooling as anywhere in Italy. Nevertheless Boccaccio's conscious advocacy is an important influence in the development of both vernacular and Latin letters. Less original than the two men whom he most admired, Dante and Petrarch, his life has striking parallels with them. Like Dante he was a layman,[1] like Petrarch he was a merchant's son. He followed Petrarch in rebelling violently against being put to learn law. Like both he knew long periods away from his native town (born in Paris in 1313 of a French mistress of his father,[1] he spent at least eight years and perhaps twice as long in Naples before he returned to Florence in 1340); and like both he was a dedicated poet. But in one important regard he differed from them. After his long and fruitful sojourn in Naples he returned to the service of his town. Of the three great Florentines, only Boccaccio really belonged to the town in daily life. This loyalty to Florence gives his whole work a completely different aspect. However much he protested his indebtedness to the Petrarch whom he regarded as his master, Boccaccio repaid the debt by making Petrarch's whole work part of the Florentine inheritance. He died in 1375, a year after his friend.

Boccaccio—and here we have a further resemblance to

[1] This has been questioned.

his exemplars—made his reputation as a writer of Tuscan, in which he composed much poetry and the first vernacular prose masterpiece, the *Decameron*: Latin, like the others, he reserved for treatises of a scholarly character. Of the influence of his vernacular poems and of the *Decameron* it is superfluous to say much. The grave beauty of his Italian immediately commanded attention and the art of the *Decameron* was humanized by the traditional nature of most of the tales and by the modern flavour the author gave them by employing as characters the persons of well-known contemporaries or near-contemporaries.[1] It is, however, in the Latin works, above all in the *De genealogiis deorum gentilium*, that we see the Petrarchan spirit vulgarized. This big collection of classical mythology was totally different from Petrarch's brilliant essays. Its humble task of diffusing knowledge helpful to the understanding of ancient poetry was however a necessary one if Petrarch's enthusiasm was to be absorbed. And on top of that the defence of poetry, undertaken by Mussato and by Petrarch, was given a most prominent place. All the old arguments are here: that the Bible is itself poetry, that poetry is divine, that it excites to virtue rather than to vice, that it despises the gaining of wealth and aspires to glory; but they are expressed with a warmth and eagerness which was to dominate all later argument on the subject. Boccaccio was a bridge between Petrarch and Florence—and one (we may remember) which influenced Petrarch as well as Florence.[2]

[1] See V. Branca's edition of the *Decameron*, 2 vols., Florence 1951–2.
[2] G. Billanovich, *Petrarca Letterato*, I, Rome 1947, pp. 59–294, 'Il più grande discepolo'.

When Boccaccio died in 1375 little seemed on the surface to have changed. In fact it is from this date that the seed sown by Petrarch and his predecessors began to bear fruit. In 1378 came the final challenge of the proletariat in Florence, the revolt of the Ciompi with its short-lived success, and then a period of relative social stability under the dominance of aristocratic families. Luigi Marsili, the Augustinian monk whom Petrarch saw as his successor in the fight against godless science of the Averroist stamp, was at Santo Spirito from 1382, the centre of a group of very diverse men who continued the old debates over moral questions and the place of literature in life. And from 1375 the Florentine chancellor was Coluccio Salutati, educated at Bologna, but a disciple of Petrarch and Boccaccio and the most vehement Florentine patriot of all. With these men and their friends, with the teaching of Giovanni di Conversino and Giovanni Malpaghini, we enter into a new phase, where the hesitant beginnings of a novel attitude give way to conviction: this will be the theme of the next chapter. Before ending this, however, there are two questions which must briefly be touched on: what consequences, if any, did the developments we have been considering have for Italy, and for political life within Italy? how far do the intellectual changes we have recorded find an echo in art?

There is no doubt that in the fourteenth century we meet a self-conscious 'Italy' more than is the case earlier. We must nevertheless be very guarded in assuming any general connection between the apostles of literature and a national revival, and equally we must hesitate to attribute too great an importance to literary programmes. In 1331 a bull, pretending to be authenticated by Pope John XXII, began to circulate in Italy. It began by rehearsing the enormities perpetrated in Italy by Roman emperors down to Henry VII, and then proceeded by the exercise of the papal plenitude of power to divide Italy from the empire ('separamus, dividimus, per partes scindimus')—thus anticipating the lengthy travail of the nineteeth century. Who put these words into the mouth of a French pope? No less a person than Robert of Anjou, king of Naples and lover of letters; indeed we might guess its French, even its Angevin origin, from a further passage where the pope, by yet another dramatic gesture, is made to limit the Franco-German frontier to what is called 'its well-established natural boundary' which the pope will indicate.[1] The exotic nature of this appeal to Italian sentiment is all of a piece with Robert's petition of 1313 where he stigmatized the German people as 'bound rather to the savagery of barbarism than the civilization of Christianity' as exemplified in France and Italy, and prayed for a stop to the German attempt to turn the sweet peace of Italy into bitterness.[2] Robert was an interested party. He was drawing on an old hostility between Italy and Germany and expressing it in the terms of an old identification

---

[1] The 'bull' *Ne praetereat* is printed in P. C. F. Daunou, *Essai historique sur la puissance temporelle des papes*, 2 vols., 4th ed., Paris 1818, II, 132–45; it is discussed and shown to be false by P. Fournier, *Le Royaume d'Arles*, Paris 1891, pp. 527–39.

[2] M.G.H., *Leges* IV (2), no. 1253 at p. 1372: 'gentem acerbam et intractabilem, que magis adheret barbarice feritati quam christiane professioni.... Cavendum est prudentia...quod Germana feritas inter tot reges et naciones non producat scandala et dulcedinem Ytalie in amaritudinem non convertat.' Cf. Fournier, *op. cit.* pp. 373–9.

between Christianity and civilization.[1] Here was to be one of the fields in which the new literature was to modify at any rate the vocabulary of politics: by the third quarter of the fourteenth century the Italian had grown familiar with the notion that barbarism began at the Alps.

Petrarch certainly played an important part in this: indeed it is probably his most important deliberate influence in the confused Italian scene, where so many of his interventions were rhetorical exercises for princely patrons, or platitudes.[2] His views on politics were in many ways old-fashioned: he looked to pope and emperor; he wanted not an effective ruler but a good ruler, saw political progress in terms of individual morality and was indifferent to any ultimate republican or royal affiliations. But there is no doubt of the passion with which he viewed Rome, the Latin inheritance and Italy. He stood four-square against the barbarians and the Greeks—for even at this late date Greeks were quite capable of demonstrating their cultural superiority and of regarding Italians as barbarians.[3] In Petrarch's words, 'sumus non Graeci, non barbari, sed Itali et Latini'. Christianity cannot cancel differences so profound. This attitude goes far beyond the mere recognition of Italy's boundaries and Italian self-sufficiency within the Empire, which we find in Dante. It reaches its noblest expression in the famous canzone *Italia mia*.[4] Here we are

[1] Cf. my essay 'Italy and Barbarian Europe', *Italian Renaissance Studies*, ed. E. F. Jacob, London 1960, pp. 48–68.

[2] Earlier writings on Petrarch's political ideas are referred to in the very useful survey by Rodolfo de Mattei, *Il sentimento politico del Petrarca*, Florence 1944.

[3] Setton, 'Byzantine Background', p. 54, quotes a passage where Demetrius Cydones (d. 1398) deplores this attitude in the Greeks of his day.

[4] See de Mattei, *op. cit.* pp. 40–51, 85–100; he accepts 1345 as the date of *Italia mia*, p. 114.

moved not only by an undoubted sincerity, but by the poet's recognition of his impotence to do more than portray his awareness of the tragedy.

Two years after *Italia mia* was written began the one attempt of the fourteenth century to turn this kind of reverence for the Roman past into a living reality: in 1347 Cola di Rienzo became Tribune of Rome. Cola (1313–54) was of humble origin and, like so many others, owed his ideas to his legal training as a notary. To the doctrines of civil law he added the apocalyptic traditions of Joachim of Flora, and he was undoubtedly influenced also by Petrarch, whose laureation on the Capitol in 1341 he had witnessed. What is significant in Cola's rise to power is not his oratorical and theatrical organization of the middle class in Rome against the turbulent aristocracy, but his vision of Italy and his failure to make this a reality. Of his vision of Italy there can be no doubt. The Roman people could revoke the *lex regia*. They would then proceed to the election of an emperor of their own choice, an Italian emperor. For this purpose all the citizens of Italy were Romans. A parliament was called to Rome to be attended by representatives of all Italian governments and in August 1347 Cola promulgated the decree (which precipitated papal hostility and thus prepared his own downfall) by which the sovereignty of the Roman people was proclaimed, by which every Italian city was declared to be free and Roman, and by which the election of an emperor was declared to belong to Rome and to Italy. So far so good: the Italian cities had no objection to being declared free, or even Roman. But the moment this was to be translated into deeds the true position emerged.

When the delegates in Rome were despatched to prepare for the election of their Italian emperor, the ambassadors of Florence refused to take up the flag they were required to carry, protesting that it involved a symbolical dependence of a feudal character. For the Florentines, as for other Italian men of affairs, the episode was an exotic variation on the interplay of republicanism and tyranny with which they were familiar. 'He wanted to bring all Italy under the obedience of Rome in the way of long ago', wrote Giovanni Villani. 'The enterprise was fantastic and could not endure.'[1] In the vast confusion of Italy Cola's flight in December 1347, his return and death in 1354 were matters of local interest.

Petrarch's reactions to the whole affair are very revealing. If the canzone *Spirto gentil* of about 1347 was not addressed to Cola it is none the less a challenge to which Cola responded after his fashion, just as Petrarch welcomed and encouraged Cola's initiative.[2] There was for Petrarch no contradiction between republicanism and the prince: he praised and blamed both liberty and tyranny at different times. In this he was guided by Cicero. For both writers a republican form of government might yet need a strong man to tide over a crisis: authority was complementary to self-government[3] and Petrarch's naturally aristocratic view of society inclined him to think that any community needed and produced a first citizen. The Signori among whom Petrarch passed so much of his time might indeed

---

[1] *Chron.* XII, 90: '...dicendo come volea riformare tutta Italia all'ubedienza di Roma al modo antico...la detta impresa del tribuno era una opera fantastica e da poco durare'.

[2] *Var.* nos. XXXVIII, XL.

[3] De Mattei, *op. cit.* p. 72.

be fairly regarded as illustrating this view, for they were both popularly elected and representatives of the emperor.[1] It is, however, notable that the Caesar of whom Petrarch is critical in the *Africa* and other early writings becomes a kind of hero later in the *Life*;[2] even if Caesar is not a tyrant, but *moderator rei publicae*, it was a fact that his intervention paved the way for later autocracy, and Petrarch was well aware of this.

This idealization of Italy and of the philosopher-king was in many ways a literary production. It none the less justified Petrarch's cultivation of the courts of the tyrants. Nothing is more telling than that Boccaccio, who deferred to Petrarch in nearly every question of policy and morality, should yet have been so outspoken a critic of his friendship with the Visconti. The fierce denunciation of Petrarch's decision to reside in Milan in 1353 is all the stronger since it is prefaced by an idyllic picture of their earlier contacts; it is all the more bitter since Petrarch had refused to establish himself in republican Florence. To the charge that he was voluntarily submitting himself to the yoke of servitude, that the lover of the solitary life was to be a mere courtier, Petrarch had no real answer save his own flattered pride and convenience. For him his comfort, honour and ability to write came first. For Boccaccio loyalty to Florence was in the last resort more important than loyalty to letters.[3] Yet even in the internal politics of Italy Petrarch's evocation of Italy had its part to play. In the 1370's Florence, faced by the papacy in the war of the Eight

[1] Ercole, *op. cit.*

[2] De Mattei, *op. cit.* pp. 103–28.

[3] The relevant letters conveniently gathered by G. Fracassetti, *Lettere di F. Petrarca volgarizzate*, 5 vols., Florence 1863–7, III, 457–73.

Saints, was to adopt as her own the defence of civilization against the barbarians from the North. But by that time Coluccio Salutati was chancellor and the roots of the Renaissance were pushing deeper.

The artistic development of Italy in the fourteenth century need not, I think, delay us more than a moment. The period is one in which, for the first time, we find a widespread influence from the North. Fourteenth-century Italian art becomes Gothic: Gothic in its attention to realistic detail, Gothic in its general complexity and richness. The native Romanesque and the dominant Byzantine influence of earlier days are not challenged in architecture save by the influence of the lofty pointed arch from beyond the Alps. In painting the penetration of northern styles is even more marked. The phrase with which Taine described the eighteenth century, 'Le joli est partout', has been justly applied by Georg Weise to the style of the thirteenth- and fourteenth-century painters and decorators.[1] He goes on:

To call Renaissance those first expressions of a worldly spirit in combination with a classical manner is wrong not only because we are faced in them by a movement general in other western countries ...but also because—and this is more important—this 'Gothicizing' process, this infiltration of French and chivalrous influences, continued to grow stronger as the fourteenth century went on.[2]

I do not think that we can dispute that, though we may care to try to explain it—by the foreign contacts of merchant communes, by the popes at Avignon employing

[1] *L'Italia e il mondo gotico*, Florence 1956, p. 19 (a summary, with very full illustrations, of the author's earlier work, *Die geistige Welt der Gotik und ihre Bedeutung für Italien*, Halle 1939). [2] *Ibid.* p. 20.

Simone Martini from Siena, by the Francophil policies of the Visconti. It may indeed be a factor to be taken into account in our examination of the cultural scene in general; for it seems that in art, as in letters, fourteenth-century Italy was not ready for the novelties hinted at by some of her sons. In letters, and in the arts, Italians as a whole in the fourteenth century preferred the *dolce stil novo*.

Most obvious confirmation of this is the startling gap between the remarkable development in painting culminating in Giotto who died in 1337 and the Italian masters of the early fifteenth century. Vasari himself was careful to point out that the praise he was giving even to Giotto and Andrea Pisano was strictly conditional: 'the nature of the times, the lack of artists, technical deficiences'; 'ma avendo rispetto al tempo, al luogo, al caso, alla persona fu tenuta stupenda'.[1] In fact Giotto was influential north as well as south of the Apennines, and that so much of his work was painted outside Florence (notably the splendid series of frescoes in the Arena chapel at Padua, and those at Assisi) suggests that there was nothing markedly Florentine about his painting [Plate VI]. Proud of him the Florentines were, as we can see from the *novelle*:[2] but perhaps as much because of his humour as his art. To say that Giotto's followers and later fourteenth-century painters were progressively more in line with the general development of northern art is, of course, not to deny merit of a high order to some of them: to Simone Martini's *Annunciation* at Florence, for instance, a great painting by

[1] Proemio to pt. II; ed. Milanesi, II. 203.
[2] Boccaccio's reverence is unquestioned; see Branca's note, II, 149 to VI, v; cf. Sacchetti, pp. 137–9, 165–6.

any standards [Plate VII].[1] But it *is* to say that Italian painting does not lead in an unbroken line from Cimabue through Giotto to Masaccio and the rest. It may well be that this northern influence was the only solvent for the stiff, rigid patterns of what Vasari called 'la maniera goffa greca ch'era tanto rozza'. Nor, as we shall see, was this to be the last or the least of northern contributions to the Italian cultural scene. The parallel developments in some of the arts from the late thirteenth century onwards is a reminder that we must not make too sharp an antithesis between Italy and transalpine countries, a point to be further examined in the final chapter.

It may have been noted that in this chapter I have treated the fourteenth century as though it ended in the 1370's. I hope to justify this in what follows.

[1] See the analysis of this painting in Weise, p. 86.

CHAPTER V

THE NATURE OF RENAISSANCE
VALUES IN THE FIFTEENTH CENTURY

BETWEEN 1375 and 1385 a number of events occurred which justify starting then a fresh chapter of Italian history. On 17 January 1377 Gregory XI entered Rome; he died a year later and, with the election of Urban VI in April 1378 and of Clement VII in September, the church was divided against itself. The Babylonish captivity had ended, the Great Schism had begun. Before Gregory XI returned tension between his Italian policy and Florentine interests had been mounting, to break into open war in the summer of 1375. This was the war of the 'Eight Saints', as the military council was called in Florence, and its mouthpiece was a new chancellor of the republic, Coluccio Salutati, who had been elected to his office in April 1375. It is in the next few years, and by the pen of Salutati, that Florentine liberty was equated in the city with the liberty of Italy; the war of the Eight Saints became the defence of Italy against barbarism. Finally, in 1378 Giangaleazzo Visconti succeeded as lord of his father's share in the family lands in North Italy: in 1385 he murdered his uncle Bernabò and was master of the whole of Lombardy. From this time onwards a kind of specious unity can be discerned in Italian affairs, as we shall see.

The great literary figures of the fourteenth century were

by now dead—Petrarch in 1374 and Boccaccio in 1375. Their successors are individually less celebrated, but they are more numerous. And the men of letters are now joined by a company of artists the like of which has never been seen before or since in numbers or in quality, save perhaps in the Paris of the late nineteenth century, when the styles adumbrated in Italy finally give way to a new grand manner. This then, in short, is the start of a period when, at any rate in certain respects, Italian political life has been simplified, while in cultural matters it has become richer and more varied: these questions are discussed in this chapter. This era comes slowly to an end in the late fifteenth and early sixteenth centuries, when foreign domination begins in Italy, and Italian cultural values begin to dominate the rest of Europe: this will be the subject of my two final chapters.

To say that the political situation is simplified in this time is not to say that it ceases to be involved, more especially before the second half of the fifteenth century with its wary equilibrium. Indeed the simplification before that derives from attributing perhaps undue importance to the successive threats by rulers of Milan and Naples to the maintenance of liberty in the other great states of the peninsula. There is no doubt that these threats were often taken seriously at the time: what remains essentially true of this, as of the preceding age, is that the reactions of the various governments of Italy were conditioned not by a general Italian situation but by the shifting pressure of local politics.

Nevertheless Visconti Milan was a new and striking

phenomenon.[1] Giangaleazzo Visconti united enormous territories under his control. It is true that he left largely untouched much of the old communal machinery at Milan and in other towns: perhaps this was not because he admitted its necessity as a source of his legal authority;[2] the survival and operation of the old councils and magistracies in any case greatly added to the stability of the new regime, concealing exactly what had happened. For some sort of a revolution had occurred. The stirrings of the principate are to be felt. Already when Giangaleazzo was a child he had been married to the French princess Isabella of Valois by his father Galeazzo, and from the dowry came Giangaleazzo's title count of Vertus (conte di Virtù) which he used until, in 1395, he purchased from Wenceslas and for an enormous sum the title of duke—the first of the dukes of Renaissance Italy. With this increase in family grandeur went administrative developments which matched the ever larger territories controlled by Giangaleazzo. Various councils, staffed by professional administrators, ran the central government, and the old chancery and camera were extended to deal with the greater volume of business. However tolerant the duke might be of communal organization, he was a bitter enemy of feudal and clerical immunities.[3] On the side of the former he was,

[1] Fondazione Treccani degli Alfieri, *Storia di Milano*, v (1310–92), vi (1392–1450), vii (1450–1500), Milan 1955–6, a collaborative work, goes far to replacing all earlier studies on the political and cultural sides (but not so adequately on the economic or administrative). For what follows see F. Cognasso, 'Istituzioni comunali e signorili sotto i Visconti', *ibid.* vi, 451–544; D. M. Bueno de Mesquita, *Giangaleazzo Visconti*, Cambridge 1941, is particularly valuable for diplomatic and administrative developments.

[2] Cognasso, *op. cit.* p. 467, takes issue with Ercole's view.

[3] De Mesquita, *Giangaleazzo*, pp. 53–4.

f course, in a dilemma, for however hard he strove to undermine old privileges, he was, as a kind of new feudal uperior, constantly creating them himself.[1] As for the lergy, the ducal line was more consistent. Bernabò had nce told the kneeling archbishop, 'Do you not know, ou fool, that here I am pope and emperor and lord in all ny lands and that no one can do anything in my lands ave I permit it—no, not even God!'[2] Bernabò was a ttle eccentric: his successors pursued the same policy with ess panache. Above all the *dominus*—the duke—emerged s a distant and all-powerful figure. The older term citizens' is dropped for the new-fangled phrase 'subjects' subditi Domini);[3] Giangaleazzo forbade the use of the vord 'popolo' and entry to the ducal presence was overned by elaborate court protocol.

The courtier had come. He was to stay—and indeed his is true of all the innovations of the Visconti period. Under the Sforza after 1450 the same trends continue, the ame institutions are further refined. One curiosity of Milanese practice suggests this continuity: dukes were numbered continuously on diplomas and coins, so that Francesco Sforza was *Dux Quartus*, Galeazzo Maria *Dux Quintus*, and so on.[4] Round the permanent duke one could nd did have a permanent career. There were limits to the tability thus procured and to the loyalty it attracted. Ludovico Sforza had just the same difficulties with trucu-ent and potentially disloyal vassals as the Visconti had

[1] Cf. Cognasso, p. 487: 'illi de Vicecomitibus'; a similar range of im-munities to that found in royal households in France.
[2] Quoted *ibid.* 537.   [3] *Ibid.* 475–6.
[4] See *ibid.* VII, plates on pp. 261, 282, 362, 366, 401; and so too in the titles of Decembrio's histories.

earlier experienced.[1] Nevertheless it is itself a novel and influential factor in the Italian scene. All the trappings of a court had been created.

In Naples there was already a court and had the kingdom been well-governed the brilliance of Visconti virtuosity might have been dimmed. But the anarchy in the *regno* was, almost literally, indescribable at the start of the fourteenth century under King Robert,[2] and it certainly did not improve as time went on. To the challenge from Aragonese 'Trinacria' (Sicily) was added the jealousy of the Balkan Angevins, particularly vehement when a new race of Angevins acquired a claim to the Neapolitan throne in 1381: the reign of Joanna I, much married and childless, which lasted from 1343 to 1382, was full of wars in which only a few great nobles benefited. Her death was followed by even greater chaos out of which was to emerge the energetic prince Ladislas whose reign from 1390, or rather (as a reality) from 1399, was to end abruptly in his premature death in 1414. Ladislas' success in politics outside Naples may suggest that he had mastered the *regno*: in reality a longer life would have shown how dearly he bought his liberty of action—in pardons to rebels, in careless sale of privileges, in a sadly depleted domain. Then comes the reign of the second Joanna, Ladislas's sister, with a further decline—if that was possible—into disorder, a disorder which enabled Alfonso

[1] An excellent article by D. M. Bueno de Mesquita illustrates this, 'L. Sforza and his vassals', *Italian Renaissance Studies*, pp. 184–216.

[2] Those chapters in R. Caggese's *Roberto d'Angio*, 2 vols., Florence 1921–30 discussing internal policy and conditions defeat the reader in search of a thread of coherence; as this clearly defeated the author. Cf. also B. Croce, *Storia del Regno di Napoli*, Bari 1925, chap. 1.

f Aragon gradually to establish himself as king by 1442. He too had bought his way as well as fought it; his interest lay in further conquest, not in husbanding his kingdom. Under Ferrante, who succeeded him in 1458, the rivalries of great houses, papal intrigue and foreign intervention resumed their disruptive work. All that a great Neapolitan historian could find to say of these days was that, despite the ambitions of Venetians and Turks to take the Adriatic ports, despite the popes' attempts to maintain their rights as overlords, despite the activities of condottieri trying to carve out kingdoms in the Abruzzi, the 'territorial unity was never broken'.[1]

The perpetual turbulence of Naples shows how relatively successful were the internal policies of successive dukes of Milan. The successes of their external policy are mainly to be accounted for by the disintegration of the States of the Church. Paradoxically the papacy in the fourteenth century was an efficient and indeed a model kingdom. The successors of St Peter no longer intervened in secular matters *ratione peccati* or for any other reason. The nonsense of *Unam Sanctam* and the claim of Boniface VIII to universal lordship were quietly put on one side. To compensate for this the fourteenth-century popes concentrated on their powers over the clergy. They did this, however, in a way which promoted their administrative rather than their spiritual controls. The result was that the curia maintained its bureaucratic ascendancy over the provinces of the church. Its elaborate chancery and treasury, its courts of law, its diplomatic machinery were more elaborate than those of any contemporary government, and in all

[1] Croce, *op. cit.* p. 42.

sorts of ways it was pioneering a new type of autocrati
government: the use made of the Italian banking facilitie
in Europe comes to mind, and so does the sale of office:
Yet the *curia Romana* was at Avignon: a paradox dwel
on by censorious critics such as Petrarch, who paid to
little attention to the very able way in which the Frenc
popes were served in Italy. There is no doubt that the fir:
real sketch of what was to be the permanent form of th
papal states dates from this period and from the militar
reforms of Cardinal Albornoz (1353–63). With a mixtur
of force and concession he and his successors tamed th
papal states, and when the popes finally returned to Ital
in 1377 they returned as masters of territories which—i
their strategic situation, with their relative agricultur;
wealth, not to mention their resources in good soldiers–
could have made the pope the leading political power in Italy

All of this was thrown away when the election o
Urban VI—the neurotic Neapolitan who saw as h;
enemies the cardinals who had elected him—was followe
by the election of Clement VII. From 1378 to 1409 ther
were two popes; from 1409 (when the Council of Pis
tried to end the schism by electing another) to 1417 ther
were three popes. The Council of Constance ended th
schism by electing Martin V, but it left a legacy of consti
tutionalism which led directly to the Council of Basle an
the election of the anti-pope Felix V in 1439. It was no
until the end of Eugenius IV's pontificate (1431–47) that th
papacy rid itself of the excuse for any Italian rebel to attac
the papacy as a servant or promoter of a council; it was nc
till the pontificate of the ex-conciliarist Pius II (1458–64
that it was declared anathema to appeal to a counci

Execrabilis, 1460). Hence for three generations after 1378 the papal states were the happy hunting ground of great princes like Visconti and Sforza, Ladislas and Alfonso, of republics like Florence and Venice, of lesser, indigenous clans like the Malatesta, the Montefeltro and the Bentivoglio. The fractionalization was almost total in 1417;[1] and the slow recovery of power which began under Martin V was for long at the expense of recognizing the *de facto* authorities which had established themselves.[2]

The anti-pope Felix V elected by the Council of Basle had been ruler of Savoy and his long reign (1391–1440) saw further consolidation in this mountainous principality. He maintained and extended his lands on the French side of the Alps, controlling the three passes of the Great and Little St Bernard and Mont Cenis, and in Italy he made good his claims to Piedmont and Saluzzo. All of this was governed with increasing centralization. The duke, for such he became in 1416, had a ducal council and *cour des comptes*; an Estates General was occasionally summoned; and in 1430 was issued the *Statuta Sabauda*, the framework of general law for all the dominions. It has, indeed, been argued that Amadeus accepted the pontificate from the fathers of Basle in order to control the bishop of Geneva, whose city formed an island of independence in the ducal territory. This impressive state, which was condemned by the growing power of France and the aggression of the Swiss cantons to turn increasingly to Italy, may have thus had laid before it 'its future destiny' as the land whence

---

[1] A very good picture of this in J. Guiraud, *L'État pontifical après le grand schisme: étude de géographie politique*, Paris 1896.

[2] P. Partner, *Papal State under Martin V*, London 1958.

were to come the sovereigns of united Italy.[1] But th
destiny lay far enough away. The truth was that, in takin
on the office of pope, Amadeus weakened his dynasti
aims; his son Ludovico (d. 1465) and his grandso
Amadeus IX (d. 1472) were poor creatures: French in
fluence penetrated and the divided lands were defenceles
when the fifteenth century drew to a close.

Bordering Piedmont and Lombardy, Genoa was at th
mercy of her more powerful neighbours while the in
stability of her government rendered her vulnerable t
their pressure. Scores of violent changes of governmen
have to be chronicled in the period between 1318 an
1528; no period was worse than the summer of 1393 whe
the office of doge, established in 1339 in imitation c
Venice, changed hands five times, a direct preliminary t
the surrender to France in 1396. From then onwards th
city was the victim of Angevin ambitions in Naples, c
Visconti and Sforza expansion, and its own secular strugg
with Venice. The public debt was put into the hands c
private merchants and civic policy lacked all loyalty an
cohesion, a striking contrast to the situation in the othe
great and rival maritime republic.

In Venice the vicissitudes which marked the politics c
other republics were not so much absent as contained
This was accomplished partly by constitutional and soci
devices and partly by a consistent aversion to mainlan
adventures. We have already noted that the *grassi* at Venic
called themselves nobles; more important than that, ther
were no genuine aristocrats, no *grandi*, to dispute thei

---

[1] See the excellent note (one suspects by C. W. Previté-Orton) in *Cambrid*
Medieval History, VIII, 329–30.

laims. The Doge, elected for life, saw his powers dwindle s his magnificence increased. Real power lay in the merchant nobility as a group, was secured by an elaborate nd successful use of lot and election, and was administered y effective executive committees and a professional civil ervice. The reader may be reminded of Florence: but at lorence there was no doge to symbolize the continuity f government, and at Venice there was no appeal to the people'. The solid administration, based on solid loyalty, vas devoted to the main interest of Venice, trade in the last and in the Adriatic. This involved securing the control f the Gulf; it involved a cautious protection of the narrow nainland territories. Hence not until the Visconti dominated Lombardy and threatened to control Romagna did he Republic accept the Florentine proposal for joint ction. In 1425 this step was taken and thereafter Venice's uture was tied to peninsular politics. Even then the constitution held, though subjected to new strains: by the midcentury the old term commune was dropped in favour of he mainland term *Signoria*; election of old men as doges ounteracted a tendency for greater political activity to ead to greater autocracy; the power of the state passed nore and more into the hands of the small council of the Dieci (the Ten). But the basic identity between 'nobility' s a whole and the government gave Venice by the end of he century a kind of mystical appeal to the remaining epublics of Italy.

> Venice, the eldest Child of Liberty
> She was a maiden City, bright and free...

Wordsworth's 'On the extinction of the Venetian Republic, 1802' is a reminder that the Venetians of the period

with which we are concerned were perfecting machiner
which was to function for centuries.

In Tuscany republicanism still lingered on, its roo
stronger there than anywhere else save Venice. A
Florence, which we will consider in a moment, the dri
to the lordship of a single man is the greatest single featur
of fifteenth-century developments, but we must remembe
that the process was not consummated till the sixteent
century and then not without a struggle. And we mu:
also remember Lucca, Pisa and Siena: Siena which endure
a tumultuous liberty in the fifteenth century, Pisa whic
after a century of Florentine domination could yet rise fo
her independence and hold it from 1494 to 1509, Lucc
which preserved herself miraculously from Florentin
dominion throughout the fourteenth, fifteenth and six
teenth centuries. As Machiavelli noted in his commentar
on Livy, Tuscany, where there was no disturbing mino
nobility, was a land of cities which 'either maintain thei
freedom or would like to do so', in marked contrast wit
all other parts of Italy save Venice.[1]

The threat to the liberty of Tuscany and especially t
Florence which developed in the last decades of the four
teenth century coincided with, if it did not precipitate
a new and original cultural development.[2] From 1385 t
1402 Giangaleazzo Visconti extended his domains south
ward, and by 1400 he had the nominal overlordship o
Lucca, Pisa and Siena; many towns of the papal states ha

[1] *Discorsi*, I, 55. And the use of the term 'nobility' at Venice was, as h
pointed out, really a misnomer.
[2] For what follows see Hans Baron, *The Crisis of the Early Italian Renaissanc*
2 vols., Princeton 1955, esp. I, 21–37, 317–50.

accepted him as lord; and in the summer of 1402 Florence's only ally, Bologna, was taken by the enemy. Florence lay virtually defenceless when, within two months of his success at Bologna, Giangaleazzo died on 3 September 1402. For a time the Visconti lands disintegrated. The new threat to 'liberty' came from the south, where by 1404 Ladislas of Naples had begun his successful intervention in the papal states: for the next ten years his ambitions, fortified by the conditions of the schism, knew no bounds and once more it was death which removed the danger. But, under cover of the general preoccupation with Ladislas, Filippo Maria Visconti, who had succeeded Giovanni Maria as ruler of Milan in 1412, had already begun the steady recovery of power. By 1422 he had mastered Lombardy and Genoa and in succeeding years began penetrating into Emilia. As we have seen, in 1425 the Venetians joined Florence in resisting this new danger, and in the event the bulk of the resistance to Filippo Maria was Venetian, the city being now firmly on the road to expansion in the north. The tortuous policy of the duke of Milan, the rising reputation and resources of his general and (after 1441) son-in-law Francesco Sforza,[1] coincided with the ending of the quarrel between the pope and the Council of Basle, with the re-establishment of the popes as at any rate theoretical masters of their states, and with the victory of Alfonso in Naples. A kind of temporary stalemate had been achieved by the mid-century, and, with Sforza, who became duke of Milan in 1450, pursuing a more cautious policy in association with Cosimo de' Medici, the new desire for more than a mere truce was formally

[1] Who married Bianca Maria, the illegitimate daughter of Filippo Maria.

recorded in the Peace of Lodi in 1454 and the Italian League which followed. The *Italiae potentiae*, the 'Italian Powers' (as they called themselves in the Italian League) had embarked on the hair-raising policy of equilibrium which was so striking an anticipation of later European systems of balance.[1] One consequence of the arrangement worth noting was that the twenty-five-year treaty involved continuous consultation among member governments. From this emerged the permanent resident ambassador, 'commonplace throughout Italy by 1460'.[2]

Dr Hans Baron has recently argued the extreme importance for Florentine cultural change of this period from the 1380's to the 1440's.[3] But we should remember that the danger of these successive threats to Tuscan liberty was probably exaggerated by contemporaries. Nothing is more illuminating than the will made by Giangaleazzo Visconti, which contained no hint of a deliberate hegemony over Italy, but on the contrary divided his inheritance among his children, reserving for the eldest only a preeminence, which would (one would have thought) have seemed an obvious way of ensuring disintegration.[4] One is reminded of the curious indifference to destiny displayed by Filippo Maria Visconti when he died in 1447 without having made any provision for the succession, not even apparently the malicious choice of Alfonso.[5] One is also

---

[1] The 'most holy league' is printed in Theiner, *Codex diplomaticus dominii temporalis S. Sedis*, III (1389–1783), pp. 379–86; *potentia italica*, *Italiae potentiae* on pp. 382–3.   [2] G. Mattingly, *Renaissance Diplomacy*, London 1955, p. 89.

[3] *Op. cit. supra*, p. 112, n. 2.

[4] The will was made towards the end of December 1399; cf. *Storia di Milano*, VI, 71.

[5] *Ibid.* pp. 392–3; this seems the inference from Bianca Maria's urging of Francesco Sforza to arrange for the succession in 1457, *unlike* her father.

reminded of the way Alfonso disposed of his patrimony: after painfully uniting Sicily and Naples with the crown of Aragon, at his death in 1458 he bequeathed Naples only to his bastard Ferrante while Sicily went to Aragon. Nor should we too readily assume that the ultimate success of Giangaleazzo was only snatched from him by death. We have already had occasion to note the rapidity with which towns, or the dominant faction or individual within urban communities, sought to place themselves under a lord whose star was rising: Robert of Anjou and John of Bohemia obtained this kind of overlordship as rapidly, if not more rapidly, than the duke of Milan and in their cases it meant very little. Siena, Perugia and the rest were following the traditional path of prudence when they accepted Giangaleazzo's protection.

This is, of course, hindsight. For the Florence of the last decades of the fourteenth century the danger was real enough, and in the light of it the threat of Ladislas and Filippo Maria early in the fifteenth century acquired a similar sombre significance. For two generations Florentine leadership in Tuscany, Florentine access to the sea, sometimes even the survival of Florentine independence itself, seemed to be in the balance. What exactly was the 'liberty' Florence strove to protect? What was the Florence which faced the threat of encirclement in 1400?

Florentine 'liberty' in the fourteenth century has been carefully analysed for us by Dr Rubinstein.[1] His conclusion is that *libertas* 'ranged from political independence to republican self-government. As far as Florence and the

---

[1] N. Rubinstein, 'Florence and the Despots in the Fourteenth Century', *Trans. R. Hist. Soc.*, 5th series, II (1952), 21–45.

other free Tuscan republics were concerned, the two coincided, for here political immunity went hand in hand with communal self-government....If independent government and freedom, "than which nothing is more precious and more acceptable to mortal beings", was desirable...so was liberty at home.'[1] This did not prevent Florence from coming to terms with Signori from time to time, or addressing Giangaleazzo in fulsome phrases as late as 1388,[2] or even pursuing a policy of subjecting other towns which the enemies of Florence could refer to as tyrannical in their turn.[3] But it did mean that in the fourteenth century Florentines saw Tuscany as the home of free communes 'che vivono in libertà'[4] as against tyrant-ridden Lombardy. Long before Salutati had charge of Florentine propaganda there were those, like Matteo Villani, who recalled the ancient Roman liberty, associated with Guelf loyalty, of which Florence was now the custodian.[5]

The Florence which emerged from the war with the pope (1375–8) and the rebellion of the Ciompi in 1378–81 was politically dominated by a number of oligarchic merchant families.[6] The machinery of government, based on the guilds, was now more heavily weighted than ever before on the side of the greater guilds—those in which

---

[1] Rubinstein, *op. cit.* 29–30; the quotation is from a Florentine diplomatic instruction of 1353.   [2] *Ibid.* 26.

[3] *Ibid.* 33–6.   [4] *Ibid.* 31 (1358).

[5] M. Villani, III, 1; VIII, 24, quoted *ibid.* 31–2; and see N. Rubinstein's 'Beginnings of Political Thought at Florence', *Journ. Warb. and Court. Inst.* V (1942), 198–227.

[6] R. Caggese, *Firenze dalla decadenza di Roma al risorgimento d'Italia*, 3 vols. Florence 1912–21, II, 280–2, 289–310; Curt S. Gutkind, *Cosimo de' Medici*, Oxford 1938, pp. 50–105.

the richest of the *popolani* predominated—so that by 13 they had seven of the nine places of the *signoria*. Within the ruling *grassi* no adequate means existed for sharing power (as at Venice), without recourse to violence: those that possessed the government for the time being could and did therefore do their best to prevent a rival group from ousting them. As popular government was still the basis of power, any appeal to the people—however innocent— might be the occasion for proscription. Thus the Alberti suffered their first banishment in 1387 and in 1402 the whole family was exiled. Other members of the mercantile autocracy followed and the ruling clique became ever smaller and ever more nervous of the families it had attacked, and of the population as a whole, taxed heavily not merely for the war of defence against Milan, but for the conquest of Pisa (1402–6) and other acquisitions. Now, as always in the medieval town, taxation lay at the root of political divisions. It was the merit of the faction dominating Florence that they accepted as inevitable the need for a relatively fair taxation system. The invention of the *catasto* of 1427, the decisive step in this direction, lay with Rinaldo degli Albizzi. When further internal dissension led in 1434 to the triumph of the faction of Cosimo de' Medici, this taxation policy, based on an attempt to assess and tax proportionately the wealth of Florentines from land and trade, was continued. It is this which lends un- doubted stability to the first half of the fifteenth century in Florence. The back-seat driving of Maso degli Albizzi, of his son Rinaldo, and of Cosimo de' Medici was punctuated by jealous gestures, banning this or that great man or family: but the government pursued aims that were in general popular, and it gradually evolved a fiscal policy which was normally applied for genuinely fiscal (not as is sometimes said for political) purposes and which went a long way to removing at least one excuse for popular disturbances.[1] It was in these years that the Renaissance flowered in Florence.

When we speak of the Renaissance at Florence we first call to mind (and I think rightly) some individual works of art[2] of astonishing genius—endowed with the compulsion which is the only test of great art. We think of the paintings of extraordinary originality which Masaccio produced in his brief life (1401–*c.* 1428), which anticipate—if they do not determine—the whole course of later Italian and Western painting [Plate X], and often reflect if they do not also sometimes anticipate the architecture which was soon to arise in Florence.[3] We think of Filippo Brunelleschi (d. 1446) and Lorenzo Ghiberti (d. 1455) and more particularly of that competition for the design of the door of the Baptistery which was held in 1402. We remember the 'St George' of Donatello, a copy of which is still standing four-square in the niche outside Orsanmichele, where it was erected about 1416 [Plate XI], and the 'Annunciation' in S. Croce (*c.* 1430). And at S. Croce in the cloisters stands Brunelleschi's Pazzi chapel, which

---

[1] Fiumi (*art. cit. supra*, p. 67 n. 1), pp. 459–64.

[2] I know of no adequate discussion of early Florentine art as a whole, but, as ever, the pages of E. H. Gombrich are fresh, sensitive and sensible: *The Story of Art*, London 1956, pp. 161–94.

[3] R. Pallucchini points out that this also happened in Jacopo Bellini's drawings, where he imagined (*fantasticava*) a Renaissance Venice thirty years before the city had acquired any buildings in the new style: *La civiltà veneziana del quattrocento*, Florence 1957, pp. 162–3.

began to be built as the 'Annunciation' was being carved and which, when completed in 1446, was the most complete architectural gesture in a new manner [Plate VIII]: the cool, lofty and tranquil arches were embellished by medallions by Brunelleschi himself, and by another influential contemporary, Luca della Robbia (1400–81). Merely to catalogue Brunelleschi's other buildings[1] would take us too long: let us say that he metaphorically crowned Florence with a new physical appearance as he crowned the cathedral with its superb dome (1420–34) [Plate XIII]. Styles of sculpture, painting and architecture had emerged which were to become in the course of time an academic norm lasting almost to our own day.

But this is only part of the picture: for the early Renaissance also suggests a whole range of intellectual developments.[2] Now is the time when manuscripts of Latin and Greek classics are collected as never before.[3] Petrarch and Boccaccio were pioneers in this, but their work, and the assiduous efforts of Poggio, were harvested by a group of scholarly bibliophiles at the centre of which stood Niccolò de' Niccoli.[4] A man of small independent means, discreetly augmented by his wealthier friends, he accumulated a collection of 800 volumes by the time he died in 1437; he also collected maps, coins and gems, and his books and his home were the centre of groups of scholar-businessmen, scholar-priests, scholar-administrators. Of

[1] E.g. the Innocenti, S. Lorenzo, S. Spirito, the Pitti palace.
[2] See in general for what follows Voigt, *op. cit.* I, 157–410.
[3] R. Sabbadini, *Le scoperte dei codici latini e greci ne' secoli XIV e XV*, 2 vols., Florence 1905, 1914.
[4] 'Il grande, l'appassionato ricercatore, il raccoglitore geniale', Sabbadini, I, 53.

the first category we may instance Giannozzo Manetti, merchant, philosopher, theologian, philologist (d. 1459); of the second, Ambrogio Traversari, a poor scholar who rose to be general of the order of Camaldoli in 1431 and who has recently been beatified (d. 1439); and of the administrators we must mention the three successive chancellors of the republic, Salutati, Leonardo Bruni, and Poggio. These are only a few names out of many. And what makes this galaxy significant is that, though as we have seen Florence had flourishing schools, it had no very successful university.[1] Founded, or perhaps refounded,[2] in 1349, it led a struggling existence, despite moments of grandeur such as when Chrysoloras taught from 1397 to 1400, or Guarino da Verona from 1411 to 1414. Other great men came and went: Aurispa (1424), Filelfo (1429–34), Giovanni Argiropulo (1456). Discontinuity such as this in Florentine higher education lends support to Poggio when he argues that great scholars are self-taught.[3] He might have added that if there was little consistent formal education in literature, there was plenty of contact between those interested. It is in the year 1389 that Giovanni da Prato puts his *Paradiso degli Alberti*, that curious mixture of stories and discussions on moral themes, told in the gardens of the Alberti mansion on the edge of Florence.[4] In this group, apart from Coluccio Salutati, the most important figure is Luigi Marsili, a Paris-trained theologian whom Petrarch regarded in some ways as his

---

[1] Voigt, I, 367.   [2] Rashdall, II, 48.

[3] Voigt, *loc. cit.*

[4] The real date for the work has been shown to be 1425–6 by H. Baron, *Humanistic and Political Literature in Florence and Venice at the beginning of the Quattrocento*, Cambridge, Mass. 1955, pp. 13–17; id. *Crisis*, I, 68–77.

spiritual heir and who, as prior of the Augustinian Hermits, turned S. Spirito into another centre of meetings for the lively and learned coteries of Florence.

In the last years of the fourteenth and in the first half of the fifteenth century these men did much to give life to the programme of Petrarch: they actively pursued classical studies for their moral guidance, for their practical importance, for their inspiration in both the fine arts and in literature. Such an ambition might fairly be described as to make life here below worthy of a creative God. I do not think one can positively explain such a development, for all explanations tend to explain away. But we are compelled to ask ourselves how it came about that Florence at this period was so vigorously set on new ways.

In Voigt's words, Coluccio Salutati secured for the new attitude to life and learning 'a right of citizenship'.[1] In place of the cosmopolitanism of Petrarch we have a spirit localized, rooted in Florence, pulsing with actuality and entirely relevant, as Dr Baron has shown in his masterly studies, to the preoccupations of the hour.[2] However accidental may have been Salutati's election to the office of chancellor,[3] he held it from 1375 to his death in 1406. His scholarship was, though in many ways traditional, yet firmly wedded to the humanities. He was the cultural

---

[1] 'Salutato hat dem Humanismus im Staatsleben das Bürgerrecht erworben', I, 161.

[2] Baron, *Crisis, passim.*

[3] Demetrio Marzi, *La cancelleria della repubblica fiorentina*, Rocca S. Casciano 1910, pp. 113–17. He was presumably appointed because of his wide experience as a notary in public office elsewhere; but when he was granted citizenship, a signal honour he was given in 1400, it was stated to be especially as a fine writer: 'Considerantes virtutum merita et scientiam eminentem, qua, *presertim rhetoricis et arte dictaminis*, in pluribus aliis pollet vir egregius', etc., *ibid.* p. 147 n.

inspiration of younger men. His reputation latterly was so great that he turned the chancellorship into a post fit for princes of learning. And his pen was ever the eloquent servant of the state. This was not achieved overnight. Salutati was a Florentine by adoption, and one of his earliest exercises was to provide Giangaleazzo Visconti with a reasoned defence of his action in murdering Bernabò in 1385.[1] But as the city grew conscious of the magnitude of the Visconti threat Salutati's letters and other writings gave the city one of its great defences. His theme was the old Florentine theme of liberty. But now liberty was proclaimed with all the force of antique precept: Florence was the city where Italian liberty had its ultimate bastion, and the inheritor of the liberty of Republican Rome; founded before the Caesars, it had all the virtue necessary to resist the Caesarian ambitions of the Milanese tyrant. Florence, the land of Dante, Petrarch and Boccaccio, was the incarnation of all that was truest and finest in the Italian tradition.[2]

The appeal of this to the civic pride of the Florentines needs little stressing. Among the younger scholars like Bruni and Poggio it struck an answering chord. The first great work of Leonardo Bruni was his *Dialogi* (ad Petrum Paulum Histrum) of 1401–5 in which Salutati is one of the speakers,[3] and in the *Laudatio florentinae urbis* (1403–4) Salutati's exaltation of the town in the 'Invective against Loschi'[4] was repeated and embellished. This has its parallels

[1] C. Salutati, *Epistolario*, ed. F. Novati, 4 vols. (Fonti per la Storia d'Italia), II, 146–59 (25 Oct. 1385). Novati argues that Salutati's letter was an attempt by the town to have Giangaleazzo as a friend rather than as an enemy, p. 146 note.

[2] See the extracts from 'Invectiva in Antonium Luschum vicentinum' in *Prosatori latini del Quattrocento*, ed. E. Garin, Milan 1952, pp. 8–36.

[3] *Ibid.* pp. 44–98 (to Pier Paolo Vergerio).   [4] *Ibid.* pp. 34–6.

in medieval sources, its model in Aelius Aristides' *Pana-thenaikos*. It transcends them all. It paints the picture of a Florence symmetrically placed in the most perfect of settings, and analyses the constitution of the city with its liberty which for Florentines is essential for life.[1] Later still, from about 1415 to 1429, Bruni composed his *History of the Florentine People*, in which these themes are taken further.[2] And they are echoed later still by Poggio; they even have a relevance to Machiavelli and the Florentine republicans of the sixteenth century.[3] This sentiment of civic loyalty was deep.[4] As early as 1373 Boccaccio had been commissioned to give a public commentary on Dante's *Divine Comedy*—a practice continued for over a century; in 1396 the Signoria debated whether to seek from their resting-places the remains of Dante, Petrarch, Boccaccio and of Accursius and Zanobi da Strada for burial in the Duomo; the matter was again taken up in 1430; and in 1455 Dante's effigy was placed there. Likewise it was the Florentine government which commissioned an Italian translation[5] of Bruni's history, the original of which was kept officially in the Palazzo della Signoria.[6] Above all it was the Signoria which appointed Bruni to follow Salutati as chancellor, Marsuppini to succeed Bruni, Poggio to succeed Marsuppini. These men were less influential than Salutati became by the end of his life, though Bruni still maintained some authority in policy as well as being the

[1] Text discussed in Baron, *Crisis*, II, 454; some extracts *ibid.* II, 517–20, and a good discussion I, 163–77. (Dates here given for these works are those advanced by Baron in this work and in *Humanistic Literature*.)

[2] Ed. E. Santini, RR.II.SS., 1914–26, with a useful short introduction.

[3] Baron, *Crisis*, I, 353–4, 371–8.

[4] Voigt, I, 386–91.   [5] By Donato Acciaiuoli.

[6] V. Rossi, *Il Quattrocento*, Milan 1938, pp. 170–1.

greatest arbiter of contemporary Latinity. But progressively they became ornaments rather than instruments of Florentine policy; this had happened already with Marsuppini, appointed in 1444; Poggio in 1453 was seventy-three years old when he was elected, a shameless old cynic; Benedetto Accolti in 1458 was a discreet combination of bureaucrat and pedant. The final change comes thereafter when Bartolomeo Scala in 1464 came to the office as a mere tool of the Medici.[1]

We must not think that the Milanese accepted unanswered the attacks of Salutati and Bruni. Court poets in Pavia and Milan were singing the praises of Giangaleazzo from the start of his rule, and it was the invective against Florence of 1399 by Antonio Loschi, the Milanese chancellor, which provoked Salutati's reply. To Florence, the citadel of republican liberty, was opposed Milan, the centre of a beneficent ruler who would bring peace to Italy, a Messiah, as he was described in one poetical effusion.[2] And just before Florence began to erect the new buildings which characterized the new mood, the huge mass of the Duomo had begun to rise in Milan: its foundation stone was laid in 1386 and soon its Gothic pinacles were to symbolize not only a Visconti *manie de grandeur* willingly shared by the Milanese,[3] but a strikingly different attitude from the cool classicism of Brunelleschi [Plates VIII, IX].

If all that Salutati, Bruni and their pupils and friends had been able to show for the humanities had been their propa-

---

[1] See the useful article by E. Garin, 'I cancellieri umanisti della repubblica fiorentina', *Rivista storica italiana*, LXXI (1959), 185–208.

[2] A. Viscardi and M. Vitale in *Storia di Milano*, v, 605–13; Cognasso, *ibid.* VI, 538–42; Garin, *ibid.* 554–6. [3] *Ibid.* VI, 896 P. Mezzanotte on the Duomo.

ganda value in war and diplomacy, the revived interest in classical studies and the concomitant developments in art might soon have petered out. But, at the same time and often in the same political atmosphere, the humanist revealed in the teaching of antiquity a much greater relevance.[1] We have seen that, faced with the alternative of *otium* and *negotium*, Petrarch was still the prisoner of older doctrines of renunciation. In the next generation Coluccio Salutati had no such hesitations. Petrarch had reproached Cicero for his involvement in politics, for daring to argue that withdrawal could in itself be a form of *negotium*. For Salutati Cicero was a good and great man precisely because he had been an active citizen. And so too with Dante: in the fourteenth century he had seemed a curious combination of clerical and secular qualities;[2] now he emerges in Bruni's *Life* as the complete man—father, citizen, poet and philosopher. As a young man (says Bruni) he gave himself to 'not only literature but...other liberal studies. But for all this he did not shut himself up at ease, nor sever himself from the world':

And here let me say a word in reproof of the many ignorant folk who suppose that no one is a student except such as hide themselves away in solitude and leisure; whereas I, for my part, never came across one of these muffled recluses from human conversation who knew three letters. A great and lofty genius has no need of such inflictions.[3]

---

[1] I here refer with gratitude to two fundamental papers by Dr Baron: 'Cicero and the Roman Civic Spirit', as above, p. 82 n. 1; 'Franciscan Poverty and Civic Wealth in Humanistic Thought', *Speculum*, XIII (1938), 1–37. See also E. Garin, *L'umanesimo italiano*, pp. 51–102.

[2] Villani's surprise: 'a great scholar, albeit he was a layman'—*Early Lives of Dante*, ed. P. H. Wicksteed, London 1904, pp. 141–2.

[3] *Ibid.* pp. 117, 119–20.

Bruni wrote this in Italian, and in the vernacular the same
doctrine was preached in both Matteo Palmieri's *Della vita
civile*[1] and in L. B. Alberti's *Della famiglia*: 'piace nell'uomo
non otio et cessatione, ma operactioni et actioni'.[2] 'The
greatest philosopher must give way to the greatest captain',
as Bruni said in 1433. 'The whole glory of man lies in
activity', as Vittorino da Feltre quoted from Cicero[3] to
Ambrogio Traversari—the Camaldolese monk. With the
support of these doctrines the crippling weight of renunciation which had lain on civil consciences for a millennium
could gradually be lifted. By the mid-fifteenth century the
family man, the magistrate, the soldier, might hold up his
head. The monk no longer monopolized virtue. The stock
sermon topic, whether a merchant or a soldier was more
certain of damnation, lost its sting, though it continued
to be preached.

This enormous change in moral attitudes was to condition all sorts of other contemporary problems and not
least that particular feature of Christian abnegation which
treats of wealth. Here, too, the Bible is awkward: 'If thou
wilt be perfect, go and sell that thou hast and follow me';
'It is easier for a camel to go through the eye of a needle
than for a rich man to enter into the kingdom of God'.[4] So
vehemently had this been accepted by earlier ages that the
whole physical landscape of Christendom was altered by
it: the great monasteries with their huge estates are testimony to the guilty consciences of generations of lords,

[1] 'Scrittori politici italiani, 14', ed. F. Battaglia, Bologna 1944, *passim*.
[2] *Ed. cit.* p. 193.
[3] *De off.* I, vi; W. H. Woodward, *Vittorino da Feltre and Other Humanist
Educators*, Cambridge 1897, p. 82.
[4] Matt. xix. 21, 24; Luke xviii. 22, 25.

he myriad churches of the towns witness to the concern
of the urban classes. The position was more awkward in
taly than elsewhere partly because of the great commercial
wealth of certain towns and partly because the call of
St Francis was still echoing in men's minds. What could
he anxious merchant do? He could be buried in the habit
of one of the mendicant orders; he could open a page in
his ledger for 'il conto di messer Domeneddio' and devote
one per cent of his turnover to charity.[1] Or he could listen
to the handful of scholars who told him that his guilt was
needlessly felt. The humanist here was not so ready with
a response at first. Salutati, like Petrarch, advocated a kind
of stoic indifference to worldly fortune, and in the republican writers most admired, like Cicero, the emphasis was
also on the simple life, on *paupertas*, for in the dying Roman
Republic an earlier austerity seemed the ideal:

> Happy the man whose wish and care
> A few paternal acres bound.

to Horace as paraphrased by Pope;[2] and Tacitus in the
Germania said much the same thing with more asperity.
It was, in fact, through the pages of Aristotle that Leonardo
Bruni found a way out of the dilemma. The pseudo-
Aristotelian *Economics*, which Bruni translated in 1419–20
for Cosimo de' Medici, led him to the comment that 'the
possession of external goods "affords an opportunity for the
exercise of virtue"'; in Martial Bruni found the observa-
tion that penury can restrict a man's virtues; and in
Aristotle's *Nicomachean Ethics* he found liberality involved

---

[1] Y. Renouard, *Les Hommes d'affaires*, pp. 185–6.
[2] Pope 'on Solitude'; Hor. *Epod.* ii. 1: 'Beatus ille qui procul negotiis'.

in virtue, and virtue thus involved in material possessions.[1] Others took up the theme. Manetti showed how Boccaccio's advocacy of poverty had been a hindrance to his intellectual progress; Alamanno Rinuccini showed that Matteo Palmieri's life had been deliberately devoted to a careful husbandry in order to provide for 'a brilliant life, for fame, for ever-increasing honours, for magnificent buildings, for his personal needs as well as for foundations in honour of God'.[2] The message is indeed already in Palmieri's *Della vita civile*,[3] and we find it too in Alberti: increasing possessions are an important ingredient in family happiness; wealth is the source of friendship and praise, of fame and authority in the individual as it is in the prosperity of the state; a family must erect and decorate buildings, possess beautiful books and fine horses.[4] A man, concludes Alberti, needs three things: 'la casa, la possessione, et la bottega'; the question is only whether his main wealth should be cash or land.[5] Here, too, in the second half of the fifteenth century the man of wealth, like the man of affairs, had found a justification, and he had found it in the company of the scholars and their books.

The contrast between these new attitudes and those of traditional Christian teaching was, of course, obvious and one may wonder why the total rejection of Christianity did not follow. It did not. The alleged atheism of Poggio and Marsuppini has too slender a basis for acceptance.[6]

[1] Baron, 'Franciscan poverty', pp. 20–1.
[2] *Ibid.* 22–3.   [3] *Ed. cit.* pp. 118–21, 128–31, 146–7, 154.
[4] *Della famiglia*, pp. 153, 210, 330–1.
[5] *Ibid.* pp. 332, 390–7.
[6] On C. Marsuppini (d. 1453) and his supposed rejection of Christianity see P. G. Ricci, 'Una consolatoria inedita del Marsuppini', *Rinascita*, III (1940) 387. For a further note on religion see below, pp. 165–7.

V   THE PIAZZA DEL MERCATO, LUCCA

VI   GIOTTO, 'THE ANNUNCIATION TO ST ANNE'

VII MARTINI, 'THE ANNUNCIATION'

VIII   THE PAZZI CHAPEL, FLORENCE

IX   THE DUOMO, MILAN

X   MASACCIO, 'ADAM AND EVE EXPELLED'

XI DONATELLO, 'ST GEORGE'

One suspects that genuine indifference to religion was both exceedingly rare and far more likely to be found in the mercantile class than among scholars;[1] certainly an avowed anti-clericalism (which as I have already said is not the same as atheism) is abounding in both scholar and merchant —and (again to repeat) in many clergy; of the so-called paganism which followed on the revival of letters I shall say a word later.[2] But it is more important, in reflecting on the religious implications of these changes in moral theory, to recall that in many ways the humanist was re-evoking certain attitudes which had been largely hammered out by earlier theologians. For example, Bruni's attitude to wealth is quite compatible with the Thomist position,[3] and Archbishop Antonino of Florence (d. 1459) made this very plain in his *Summa*.[4]

Another danger in viewing these developments at Florence is to assume that the whole of the governing class was devoted to the new learning. This was far from being the case. We now know better than to argue that the scholars whose names have so often occurred in this chapter were neglectful of the vernacular and so out of touch with popular movements of opinion. This used to be advanced as the most serious criticism of the reverence for the humanities in the Quattrocento. On the contrary, nearly all the great Latin scholars of the Quattrocento also wrote in Italian—or at Florence in Tuscan. And there is no doubt that the influence of Latin on the vernacular at this time was to be beneficial however laboured the results

---

[1] This is certainly the impression one gets from the novelists.
[2] Below, pp. 175–6.
[3] Baron, 'Franciscan poverty', p. 21.
[4] Garin, *L'umanesimo italiano*, p. 88.

sometimes were.[1] Yet even if we accept this, we must also accept that the men who were influential in Florence were not all like Palla Strozzi or Cosimo de' Medici. Vespasiano da Bisticci, the Florentine bookseller (1421–98) whose *Lives* provide an unaffected picture of his friends and customers, writes of Andrea de' Pazzi as a typical merchant 'who thought learning to be of little value and had no desire that his son (Piero) should spend time over it'. He also shows us more than once a tongue-tied, semi-literate Signoria at the mercy of a fluent humanist diplomat.[2] And Alberti in no uncertain terms condemns the indifference to literature of the Florentines of his own day. Florentines, he says, are not interested in the liberal arts; in aiming at wealth they end up commonly by being ill-educated; 'they say it is enough to be able to sign your own name and be able to strike the balance in a ledger'.[3] And there was a deeper popular current which was not merely indifferent but hostile to the scholarship of the few.[4] It has been argued that the mockery to which many learned men of the old order were exposed—notaries, doctors, teachers —made the rhymesters who recited at S. Martino the allies of the exponents of the new humanities: both were contemptuous of the Latinizing of those who wrote vernacular prose and poetry under the influence of Petrarch and his successors. But it seems far more likely that Filippo

---

[1] There is a very big literature on the subject; see C. Grayson, 'Lorenzo, Machiavelli and the Italian Language', *Italian Renaissance Studies*, pp. 410–32 and references, especially in early pages.

[2] *Lives*, ed. Waters, pp. 310, 150, 321, 387.

[3] *Op. cit.* pp. 60–1; cf. 388 ff. for the two kinds of learning, experience and books.

[4] See in general V. Rossi, *Il Quattrocento*, Milan 1938, pp. 218–80; and D. Guerri, *La corrente popolare nel rinascimento*, Florence 1931.

Villani and Domenico da Prato were ruffled by these often scurrilous attacks because they were representatives of the classical trend, in both Latin and vernacular, who were accessible to the people—as the mainly Latin-writing Salutati and Bruni were not.[1]

There was, however, a deeper sense in which the changes we have considered *were* in tune with the popular spirit. The whole trend of humanist speculation in Florence in the early fifteenth century was towards an accommodation with the here-below, and a rejection, implied and sometimes explicit, of the abnegation hitherto officially associated with transcendental religion. The monks and priests who for hundreds of years had voiced for all men the ideals of an ascetic Christianity were now joined by apostles of a different stamp. Worldly success, worldly wisdom, worldly virtue were advanced as rivals to the way of mortification. This (so far as one can judge) had been in practice how most ordinary men thought about their earthly pilgrimage: it was now a respectable position. And something similar had happened in fine art. The realism which we find in certain aspects of late Gothic, and which emerges triumphant in Masaccio, was at any rate how many men had for long pictured the world to themselves. 'The Brancacci Chapel, where the Renaissance learned how to paint, owes nothing to the Greeks and the Romans.'[2]

It is tempting to date from the early fifteenth century not only the fundamental alterations in moral values which

[1] Cf. Guerri, pp. 85–8.
[2] Guerri, p. 103; cf. p. 47. And cf. also Weise, *L'Italia e il mondo gotico*, p. 37. But, even if we accept this, it remains true that the 'popular' in Italy was tinged—if not more deeply dyed—with the colours of the Roman world.

have been described, but others. We have been accustomed by a century of scholarship to view the Renaissance as the birth of modern civilization, and this Burckhardtian tradition is in a way compatible with what we have so far disentangled from the changing patterns of ideas. Clearly in certain fields of sentiment and representation of sentiment the humanist position towards the active life inevitably carried with it consequential readjustments. Far and away the most important of these was an entirely novel attitude to education, about which I shall say more later. With this we may link the changes which have been acutely observed in the 'secularization of wisdom'[1] and, though its course is less well plotted, with new principles in political and constitutional thought.[2] The whole range of literature, the subject about which we know most, was enormously extended.[3] One kind of literature, artistic prose and poetry, took on fresh forms which themselves condition our very apprehension of the period with which we are concerned. The writing of history after Bruni was quite a different matter, not merely because he provided (on the inspiration of antiquity) a new narrative form and (despite the admiration of antiquity) a new seriousness in regard to the treatment of his sources, but because he made the writing of history a factor in politics, and because (this is the really important thing) he taught his con-

---

[1] Eugene F. Rice, Jr., *The Renaissance Idea of Wisdom*, Cambridge, Mass. 1958, esp. pp. 30–57; cf. H. Baron's 'review-discussion' in *Journ. Hist. of Ideas*, XXI (1960), 131–50.

[2] Partial discussions in essays by N. Rubinstein (above, pp. 115–16nn.). The Italian approach to political speculation is (like so much French writing on the subject) disastrously dominated by the lawyers, so becoming schematic and unhistorical.

[3] V. Rossi, *Il Quattrocento* and G. Toffanin, *Il Cinquecento*, both *passim*.

temporaries to look at the past *as* the past: he sliced time up in quite a new way.[1] These are all innovations of the greatest importance and all can fairly, I believe, be placed to the credit of the early Quattrocento in Florence.

But there are equally significant zones of speculation and action where we must reject attempts to attribute originality of this order to early Renaissance Florence. This is perhaps most clearly the case in philosophical studies. The question has been much debated.[2] The truth of the matter seems to be twofold: on the one hand the influence of the revived classics made less impression in metaphysical speculation because the main Greek texts were very old friends and all that humanists did was to provide better versions;[3] and on the other hand humanists of the first generation were not particularly inclined to philosophical enquiry as such, even if very few shared to the full the professed hatred of the Ockhamist or the Averroist which is supposed to be characteristic of the Renaissance scholar. For a time at any rate questions of a metaphysical and theological nature were not the concern of the pacemakers: they were running a different race.

One aspect of the philosophical problem needs a further word: physical science. For those who follow Burckhardt this too is a conquest of the Renaissance; for those who wish to ensure continuity in scientific progress the Renaissance is naturally cast for a leading role. I am convinced

[1] With all its manifest faults (arising from an *a priori* approach) the best general work is still E. Fueter, *Geschichte der neueren Historiographie*, best read in the (revised) French translation of E. Jeanmaire, Paris 1914; the Italian trans. (2 vols., Naples 1944) has an appendix of additional references.

[2] E.g. by Gentile, Saitta, Garin, Kristeller and others; see the bibliography in E. Garin's *L'umanesimo italiano*.

[3] And sometimes versions which were too free for scholarly use.

that this cannot be sustained. Physical science in the later middle ages is not dead. It lives steadily on, but in the older centres like Paris and Oxford which are not affected by Renaissance innovations until much later. Petrarch's attacks on Averroists are, on the other hand, not to be taken as constituting an explanation of the Renaissance, though Giuseppe Toffanin has often brilliantly so argued:[1] the significant figures of the Renaissance, so it seems to me, were neither for nor against physical science. They were as relatively indifferent to this particular aspect of traditional philosophy as to philosophy of the old kind altogether. When philosophy did emerge as a Renaissance interest it was to be (as we shall observe) a 'love of wisdom' different indeed from the traditions of the medieval university, but even less relevant to the mathematicians and the physicists and the chemists.[2]

One solitary exception must now be made to this general judgment: optics and perspective. Here theory marched with practice.[3] Brunelleschi's and Alberti's studies on perspective matched a lively empirical approach which is found not only in Italy but also in Flanders. And as a result of their work formulae could be provided for the painter and architect which enabled them, merely by

[1] Notably in *Che cosa fu l'umanesimo*, Florence 1929, and in *Storia dell'umanesimo*.

[2] The debate on the place of science which is to be found in *Journ. Hist. of Ideas*, IV (1943), is important, and in particular Dana B. Durand's essay, pp. 1–20, is worth looking at.

[3] See J. Schlosser, *Die Kunstliteratur*, Vienna 1924, pp. 105–12, 120–30. Useful passages from Antonio Manetti's *Life of Brunellesco* are given in Elizabeth G. Holt, *Literary Sources of Art History*, Princeton 1947, pp. 95–107; see esp. pp. 97–9. For the empirical approach see John White's two papers in *J. Warb. and Court. Inst.* XII (1949), and XIV (1951); there is a big and growing literature on the whole subject.

following certain rules, to make a plane surface carry the illusion of three dimensions, and which could make architecture both the vehicle of other illusions and the corrector of optical distortions. The proofs of the importance of these scientific advances are still with us. For relevance and applicability these achievements are of far greater importance than all the intuitions and ambitions buried out of sight in Leonardo da Vinci's notebooks. It is not a great march forward on the road of science: but it is a real one.

In this chapter the word humanist has been used a good deal. I have felt this justified because it presumably comes into the student slang where it was born about the mid-fifteenth century, though the earliest instance so far recorded dates from 1490.[1] The *umanista* was a teacher of the *studia humanitatis*, the old grammarian, the arts professor. His range of interest has been described thus:

The *studia humanitatis* came to stand for a clearly defined cycle of scholarly disciplines, namely grammar, rhetoric, history, poetry, and moral philosophy, and the study of each of these subjects was understood to include the reading and interpretation of its standard ancient writers in Latin and, to a lesser extent, in Greek. This meaning of the *studia humanitatis* remained in general use through the sixteenth century and later....[2]

Even by the end of the fifteenth century, the *umanista* was often a pretty unexciting pedant. His early fifteenth-

---

[1] A. Campana, 'The Origin of the Word "Humanist"', *Journ. of the Warb. and Court. Inst.* IX (1946), 60–73, with the appended note on Kristeller's discovery of the Pisan text of 1490. *O.E.D.* records the first English use of 'humanist' in this sense in 1589.

[2] P. O. Kristeller, *Classics and Renaissance Thought*, p. 10.

century predecessors were, in some cases, very remarkable men. So well known, not least from the excellent books by W. H. Woodward,[1] are the schoolmasters of early Renaissance Italy that it is not necessary to labour their originality or their influence. After the rather dimmer figures of Conversino and Malpaghini at the end of the fourteenth century and Gasparino Barzizza a little later, Guarino da Verona and Vittorino da Feltre stand out in clear relief, the schoolmasters of many influential men, above all the schoolmasters of other teachers. Their exemplification of the *vita activa*, against the clerical ideal of earlier education, is evident in all they did; their teaching is worth all the many theoretical treatises of the fifteenth century,[2] important as they are and in agreement with the very practical aims of the teacher. 'Not everyone', said Vittorino, 'is called to be a lawyer, a physician, a philosopher, to live in the public eye, nor has everyone outstanding gifts of natural capacity, but all of us are created for the life of social duty, all are responsible for the personal influence which goes forth from us.'[3] Rhetoric and letters were the means for educating a citizen, Latin was the means to virtue in a completely balanced personality.

It may well seem odd to introduce Vittorino and Guarino in an account of cultural developments at Florence. The answer is that the two men had adopted views first

---

[1] *Vittorino da Feltre*; *Studies in Education during the Age of the Renaissance*; R. Sabbadini, *Il metodo degli umanisti*, Florence 1922; E. Garin, *L'educazione in Europa 1400–1600*, Bari 1957.

[2] A useful list in Woodward, *Vittorino*, pp. 180–1; a good collection of extracts in E. Garin, *L'educazione umanistica in Italia*, Bari 1949.

[3] Quoted by Woodward, *Studies*, pp. 12–13.

completely expressed in the circle of Salutati and Bruni. Here, for example, is the concluding portion of Bruni's short treatise on education:[1]

That high standard of education to which I referred at the outset is only to be reached by one who has seen many things and read much. Poet, orator, historian and the rest, all must be studied, each must contribute a share. Our learning thus becomes full, ready, varied and elegant, available for action or for discourse in all subjects. But to enable us to make effectual use of what we know we must add to our knowledge the power of expression.... Proficiency in literary form, not accompanied by broad acquaintance with facts and truths, is a barren attainment; whilst information, however vast, which lacks all grace of expression, would seem to be put under a bushel, or partly thrown away.... Where, however, this double capacity exists—breadth of learning and grace of style—we allow the highest title to distinction and to abiding fame.... My last word must be this. The intelligence that aspires to the best must aim at both. In doing so, all sources of profitable learning will in due proportion claim your study. None have more urgent claim than the subjects and authors which treat of Religion and of our duties in the world; and it is because they assist and illustrate these supreme studies that I press upon your attention the works of the most approved poets, historians and orators of the past.

All that Bruni here says is also to be found in two vernacular treatises by Florentines: Matteo Palmieri's *Della vita civile*[2] and L. B. Alberti's *Della famiglia*.[3] That these Florentine notions were not uniquely Florentine and that they were to be reinforced indeed by non-Florentine elements is a matter to which I shall draw attention in my next chapter.

[1] This is translated in Woodward, *Vittorino*, pp. 132–3; composed between 1423 and 1426, according to Baron, *Crisis*, ii, 613–14.
[2] *Ed. cit.* pp. 36–9; cf. above, p. 11.
[3] *Ed. cit.* book i, *passim*.

I will conclude this chapter by coming back once more to Italy as a whole and to the Florentine position in Italy. Two points may have suggested themselves during the previous discussions: first, that the republicanism so characteristic of Florentine attitudes was something not (to put it mildly) found everywhere in Italy; second, that in Florence itself republican realities were doomed to decline in the second half of the fifteenth century and to disappear early in the sixteenth.

It will be remembered that in 1347 Cola di Rienzi summoned all Italians to join Rome: to be under the leadership of a Rome which extended Roman citizenship to the whole of the peninsula. And it will be remembered that Florence was hesitant and suspicious in reacting to this offer. The tables were turned in 1375. The stirring call to liberty which Florence sounded in the papal states led to the rebellion of the Romagna and spread to the Patrimony. But to the appeals sent to Rome the Romans turned a deaf ear: just as it suited towns like Perugia and Bologna to proclaim popular government, so it suited the Romans to welcome back the pope. But what of the other *republics* at this moment when Florence in her war with Giangaleazzo sought to defend the threatened liberty of Italy? The Tuscan republics were more frightened of Florence than of the ogre in Milan;[1] Venice was a lukewarm ally for a while but played for time. Meanwhile Florence in desperate straits sought to defend the liberty of Italy by provoking the armed intervention of Rupert of Bavaria, elected emperor in 1400: Giangaleazzo when he had pushed the German back could claim with some reason that he and

---

[1] Cf. Bueno de Mesquita, *Giangaleazzo*, pp. 247–8.

not Florence was the protector of Italy, having chased away 'those barbarian nations, enemies of Italy, against whom the Alps themselves had been placed by nature as a bulwark'.[1]

Nor was Florence the only commune to frighten her neighbours into accepting the alliance or the lordship of a tyrant. Venice in and after the second quarter of the fifteenth century is equally dangerous. As early as 1449 Venetians could be accused of seeking to be 'Signori di tutta Italia'.[2]

No generalized republican sentiment was in fact conceivable in fifteenth-century Italy: the name Italy is bandied about as never before; barbarians are more frequently identified and stigmatized. But liberty was a local liberty and a town would rather submit to a tyrant unwillingly than voluntarily sustain republican ideals by adherence to a republic: this the Milanese learnt sharply when in 1447 all the towns controlled by the Visconti deserted the Ambrosian Republic.

The Ambrosian Republic came into being at Milan on the death of Filippo Maria Visconti, very largely because the duke, deceitful and suspicious to the end, left no instructions regarding the succession. The facility with which the commune re-emerged after a century of subjection to Visconti rule is striking evidence of the continued functioning of communal institutions and of their importance as a source of power;[3] but beyond that the cry of 'libertade' was, one need hardly say it, the cry of a faction: and one

---

[1] Quoted Simeoni, *Signorie*, I, 213; cf. Bueno de Mesquita, pp. 309–10.

[2] F. Sforza to Cosimo de' Medici, 23.10.1449: Simeoni, I, 530, n. 6.

[3] Cf. Ercole's thesis, above p. 64.

which was raised in other towns dominated by the Visconti, as has just been said.[1] It was a faction to which the humanist Pier Candido Decembrio served as a mouthpiece: he remained secretary to the new Signoria as he had been the secretary and chronicler of the dead duke; and as he was to be prepared, even anxious, to serve the new duke, Francesco Sforza, who established himself in 1450. Decembrio's presence at the centre of action has led to an assumption that the revived commune was humanist-inspired; he has been treated rather as the Salutati of the episode. There seems no doubt that he preferred communal liberty to ducal government, despite what looks like time-serving behaviour,[2] and his letters seeking an alliance for the town in 1448-9 roused the anger of Sforza's supporters in much the same way as Salutati's had angered the Visconti half a century earlier.[3] But it has been justly said that he did not really have faith in republican principles,[4] and Filelfo, who happened to be there at the time, was a very unwilling collaborator—in the end helping to secure Sforza's victory. There the influence of humanists ends, and it does not amount to much: indeed if one seeks

[1] For the course of events see F. Cognasso's chapter in the *Storia di Milano*, VI, 387-448.

[2] P. C. Decembrio, *Opuscula Historica*, RR.II.SS. xx, ed. A. Butti, F. Fossati and G. Petraglione, pp. 431-7; after 1450 Decembrio was first at the papal curia, then with Alfonso; for a time he also served Borso d'Este at Ferrara; he was, somewhat precariously, in Milan for some years after 1459 and he died there in 1477.

[3] G. Simonetta, *Rerum gestarum F. Sfortiae commentarii*, RR.II.SS. xxi, ed. G. Soranzo, p. 258.

[4] A. Colombo, 'Della vera natura ed importanza dell'Aurea Repub-blica Ambrosiana', *Raccolta di scritti storici in onore del prof. G. Romano*, Pavia 1907, pp. 3-13; at p. 9 he criticized A. Butti's *I fattori della repubblica ambrosiana*, Vercelli 1891; on both see the long note in the RR.II.SS. xx, pp. 436-7.

to make this a 'revolution of the intellectuals' the lawyers are more important than the grammarians.[1] What really happened was that as the movement drifted into popular hands, the magnates of Milan were reconciled to the idea of Sforza. The events between August 1447 and December 1449 certainly show that there was in Milan a hatred of tyranny which was not just literary: but Machiavelli was surely right to instance the Ambrosian Republic as an example of a people corrupted by princely rule being unable to maintain a reacquired liberty.[2]

Even more corrupted (in this sense) and even less influenced by humanist republican ideals was the city of Rome, where Cola's gesture was, however, not forgotten. The years of the Schism (1378–1417) had seen Rome at its most turbulent—jostled by popular communal movements, by the rivalry of the great families (notably Colonna and Orsini) and by the pressure of Naples.[3] Here, too, and long before the curia was staffed by Florentine men of letters, we hear the cry 'il popolo e la libertà'; indeed it was with this ringing in his ears that Eugenius IV fled the city in 1434 to take up residence in Florence, where the new values began to spread in the papal *entourage*. More to our immediate point is the conspiracy of Stefano Porcari and the so-called conspiracy of the Academy. Porcari, who had exercised the office of magistrate in a number of Tuscan and papal towns, was a well-educated Roman who

[1] Cf. Butti, p. 13.
[2] *Discorsi*, I, ch. 17; cf. *Prince*, ch. 12 (ed. Burd, p. 258).
[3] The accounts in the older works of F. Gregorovius, *History of the City of Rome in the Middle Ages*, trans. Hamilton, 8 vols. in 13, London 1894–1902, vol. VII, pt. i, and of L. Pastor, *History of the Popes*, vols. III, IV, are still important; a recent and useful survey is P. Paschini, *Roma nel rinascimento* (Storia di Roma, vol. XII), Bologna 1940.

had never concealed his desire that Rome should enjoy the same kind of liberty as, for example, Bologna. When the Emperor Frederick III came to Rome for his coronation in 1452 Pope Nicholas V sent Porcari in honourable exile to Bologna, which at the time was under the nominal control of the papal legate Bessarion. At Christmas 1452 Porcari broke his parole, returned secretly to Rome and, with a few friends, hired a substantial number of cut-throats and soldiers for an attempt to seize power during the celebrations of Epiphany. The escape of Porcari from Bologna was learnt of and his plans revealed, and he was arrested and executed on 9 January 1453. It was a revolution which hardly even misfired, so total a fiasco was the whole sad business. For Porcari had been popular with curia and people, a good speaker, a disinterested man.[1] Equally paltry is the affair of Tiburzio di Maso in 1460, despite the prominence given to it in Pius II's autobiography: a riot of young men in search of trouble.[2] After these fruitless demonstrations one would have thought the popes would have rested content with their ever growing power in the city, and it comes as a surprise to see Paul II take so seriously both the threats of the disgruntled scholars (led by Platina), who had lost their curial employment in his economy drive, and the posturing of the antiquarians and grammarians (led by Pomponio Leto). Yet the pope did take the matter seriously. Platina, arrested in 1464, was rearrested in 1468, on charges of heresy and political conspiracy, along with a score of others including Pom-

[1] Voigt, II, 67–70; Pastor, II, 215–39.
[2] *The Commentaries of Pius II*, ed. and trans. F. A. Gragg and L. C. Gabel (Smith College Studies in History, 1937–57), pp. 349–56.

ponio Leto, who was extradited from Venice.[1] Once again the whole affair melts away to nothing: the so-called conspirators were released in 1469; the pope had said some hard things about the paganizing trend of poetical studies; and Platina enjoyed the last word with the savage picture of Paul in the *Lives of the Popes*. Platina's own picture of himself contains nothing heroic: he is concerned to show his orthodoxy and, if we believe him, was a conventional Christian who did the minimum.[2] As for Pomponio Leto, his colourful re-enactment of antiquity is not in doubt; but he was a very ineffective conspirator, if he himself really was involved. He too was apparently a conventional Christian.[3] Despite their sorry performance on these occasions, Platina and Pomponio Leto have each a small but assured place in the history of scholarship: the point I am trying to make here is how useless republican sentiment was in fifteenth-century Rome. Porcari does seem to have been genuinely fired by Florentine ideals; his nephew Tiburzio more by revenge and by astrologers; the academicians by jealousy of the pope and of each other. And (this is worth noting) none of them had really an *Italian* policy, as Cola had a century before.

The Tuscan communes were of course more attuned to the spirit of independence and its cultural manifestations and we are not surprised to find at Siena, for example, a whole political programme, tinged with the values we

[1] V. Zabughin, *Giulio Pomponio Leto*, 2 vols. in 3, Rome–Grottaferrata, 1909–12, I, 40, 99; for the connection of this affair with the 1460 troubles see I, 115–16.

[2] *Vitae*, ed. Gaida, RR.II.SS. III, pt. i, 388: 'I lived as befits a Christian and never missed confession and communion at least once a year.'

[3] Zabughin, *op. cit.* I, 53, 209–30.

associate with Renaissance Florence, being painted in the Palazzo Pubblico in 1414. These frescoes, which have been carefully analysed by Dr Rubinstein[1] and compared with another series painted seventy-five years earlier, are in their technical execution not strikingly original; but the ideas of Roman republican antiquity and of fame which they portray are probably the result of 'a direct or indirect connection with the Florentine humanists'.[2] Nevertheless that political hostility to Florence which we have already noted stood as a barrier to the reception of Florentine notions in any large-scale way: Pisa, subjugated in 1406, stood as a melancholy example of the city which failed successfully to resist Florentine ambitions. Genoa also was not receptive to the new values. Humanists there are and, as at Florence, in the office of chancellor;[3] one of them was indeed a considerable scholar—Giacomo Braccelli who exercised the office from 1431 to 1460. Yet the most recent survey of fifteenth-century Genoese culture concludes, and rightly, that 'Genoese public life was completely detached from the spirit of humanism'.[4] The solitary exception seems to be the *Laudatio Ianuensium* of Giannozzo Manetti, written in 1436 in Florence and revised in Genoa.[5] Here Florentine civic attitudes are indeed found. But Manetti was a Florentine and his doctrine did not take root in Genoa.

[1] N. Rubinstein, 'Political Ideas in Sienese Art: the Frescoes by Ambrogio Lorenzetti and Taddeo di Bartolo in the Palazzo Pubblico', *Journ. Warb. and Court. Inst.* XXI (1958), 179–207.

[2] *Ibid.* p. 203. [3] Voigt, I, 442–3.

[4] G. G. Musso, 'La cultura Genovese fra il quattro- e il cinquecento', *Miscellanea di Storia Ligure*, I (1958), 123–87, at p. 128.

[5] Baron, *Crisis*, II, 607–8; Musso, who promises an edition, gives the date for the second version as 1444, not 1437, *op. cit.* p. 124 n.

A close association between the humanities and social and political life might have been expected to develop in the remaining republic, Venice. As we shall see in the next chapter, something like this had occurred by the early sixteenth century. But in the first half of the fifteenth the fresh ideas of the Renaissance are not particularly impressive at Venice. The city was, of course, engaged in war on a scale unparalleled elsewhere in Italy, for on top of the savage rivalry with Genoa and other maritime powers, especially on the Adriatic, came the tremendous struggle with the Ottoman Turks who had dominated Asia Minor and much of the Balkans before Constantinople fell in 1453. True, a few of the 'nobles' were influenced by a new attitude to literature and philosophy: e.g. Leonardo Giustinian (d. 1446) who corresponded with Florentine scholars, and Francesco Barbaro (d. 1454). But we are struck by the way in which Greek scholars both native and Italian landed at Venice and then made rapidly for more receptive centres elsewhere. For the native Greeks, we may suppose, the trophies of the thirteenth-century conquest of Constantinople so arrogantly displayed at San Marco were not very agreeable. There seem to have been more facilities for formal education than used to be thought, but not until 1443 did the senate make provision for regular teaching of the humanities;[1] the penetration of Florentine artistic styles comes later still. As for collections of books, Petrarch's gift never materialized, and the first libraries were those provided by Cosimo de' Medici and bequeathed by Bessarion. Above all we are struck, as

---

[1] See Bruno Nardi's survey of literature and culture in *La civiltà veneziana del quattrocento*, Florence 1957, pp. 101–45.

Vespasiano da Bisticci was struck at the time, by the absence of Venetian political propaganda in the new historiographical manner.[1] Yet one remarkable piece of evidence exists for a spirit at Venice akin to that of early fifteenth-century Florence: Francesco Barbaro's *De re uxoria* (1415). This treatise on matrimony was written when he was seventeen, and as the result of a visit to Florence. But it was immensely popular and it anticipates remarkably fully the Florentine defence of wealth I have mentioned earlier.[2] In Barbaro as he grew older we also find an increasing awareness of *Italian* liberty, as contrasted with Venetian liberty.[3] But the federation of Italian republics, so fond a dream when Florence and Venice signed their alliance in 1425, so clearly reflected in Barbaro, Andrea Giuliano, and Piero del Monte,[4] was soon to be an impossibility, for Florence ceased to be a republic.

Our evidence for republican sentiment must also take into account the question of tyrannicide, to which both Machiavelli and Burckhardt devoted celebrated chapters.[5] There seems no reason to think that Italy differed significantly from the North in this matter either in the violence or frequency of assassination or in the theories used to justify or condemn it. The bad ruler was no ruler: such in brief was traditional medieval theory; resistance to a tyrant had been advocated by John of Salisbury and Thomas Aquinas. There is, however, a distinct drift away from this towards

---

[1] See extract below, p. 153.

[2] Baron, 'Franciscan Poverty', pp. 18–19. *De re uxoria* is printed by Garin in *Prosatori latini*, pp. 104–37.

[3] See Carotti, 'Francesco Barbaro', *Riv. stor. ital.* ser. 5 ii (1937), 18–37 esp. 22–4.   [4] Baron, *Crisis*, pp. 345–6, 393–4.

[5] *Discorsi*, III, 6; *Civ. of the Ren.* pt. i, ch. 6.

a doctrine which protected the prince and when, after the murder of Louis of Orleans by the duke of Burgundy in 1407, Jean Petit sought to defend the act we have a sense of anachronism. Petrarch, as we have seen,[1] felt that even in a republic there could be an occasion for a strong man and Salutati in his *De tyranno* (1400) justified Dante for putting Brutus in the bottommost pit. Yet the reinforcement of republicanism by antique precept could not fail both to rehabilitate Brutus[2] and to afford colour to conspirators anxious to justify their actions. Hence the sentiments expressed by the conspirators who murdered Galeazzo Maria Sforza in 1476: the young men who killed the duke all had private grievances against him, but they were lent inspiration and a theory by the disgruntled humanist Cola Montano. The deed itself was singularly fruitless; it is not essentially different from the attempted murder of Lorenzo de' Medici by the Pazzi in 1478; or the attempted murder of Ludovico il Moro in 1484. We should also recall that the virtue of tyrannicide was even used to exculpate the unpleasant Lorenzino de' Medici after his murder of Alessandro in 1537. The one instance of what appears to be a disinterested crime is the ill-fated conspiracy of Pierpaolo Boscoli and Agostino Capponi to murder the Medici in 1513. Yet we know how earnestly Boscoli wished, when faced with execution, to return to the old ways: what is important is not his earlier espousal of civic martyrdom but his final desire to die as a good and conventional Christian. And Boscoli was, after all, a Florentine, and thus not typical of Italy at large in this matter. As Guicciardini

---

[1] Above, pp. 97–8.
[2] Cf. below, p. 171 and plate XXII.

said, tyrannicide had been practised by 'very few who were moved solely by patriotic emotions'.[1]

I do not wish to say much here about the emerging principate at Florence. In general lines it has long been a familiar story and recently it has been excellently illustrated in R. von Albertini's important book.[2] As in many a fourteenth-century town, as in Bologna in the fifteenth century, so at Florence from the 1440's a leading family gradually made itself first necessary to, then deliberate master of, the state. When Cosimo died in 1464 the Medici were so indispensable that they survived the inept leadership of Piero de' Medici from 1464 to 1469. Under Lorenzo evolution in the direction of princely government was more rapid. Long before his death in 1492 the rest of Italy was dealing with him as Signore of Florence and, though the forms of the commune survived, even in institutions there is a move to an oligarchic basis for Medici power. What held up further advance in this direction for a time was not just the folly of Piero, Lorenzo's son, but the peculiar circumstances of the French invasion of 1494. This undoubtedly released pent-up republican emotions, and there is even an overtone of old-fashioned tyrannicide, to which I have just referred, in the decision to take from the collections of the expelled Medici Donatello's 'Judith and Holofernes' and place it in front of the Palazzo della Signoria where it still stands. The next twenty years of so-called liberty were really a demonstration of the non-

[1] *Dialogo e discorsi del reggimento di Firenze*, ed. R. Palmarocchi, Bari 1932, p. 40; the whole passage, pp. 39–41, is important.
[2] Rudolf von Albertini, *Das florentinische Staatsbewusstsein im Übergang von der Republik zum Prinzipat*, Berne 1955.

viability of both genuine republican life and of the kind of covert tyranny which had existed under Maso and Rinaldo degli Albizzi, under Cosimo and Lorenzo de' Medici. It was to these good old days that most substantial and serious Florentines turned nostalgically, or else to dreams of a constitution modelled on that of Venice. In fact real liberty was unbearably turbulent in the days (1495–8) of Savonarola, unendurably tough in those last heroic years from 1527 to 1530; equally unstable were the intervening decades when incompetent Medici government in Florence slowly re-emerged under the aegis of the Medici popes at Rome, Leo X (1513–21) and Clement VII (1523–34). What still astonishes one in sixteenth-century Tuscany is the tenacity of urban independence. Pisa clung to her liberty with tragic vigour from 1494 to 1509; Siena, torn as ever by internal dissension, yet dared to face and to defy Florence and the Spaniards from 1552 to 1555; and Lucca, although as an ever tighter oligarchy of old families, preserved her communal independence. Equally remarkable is the extraordinary awareness among Florentines of the issues at stake. Just as in the early fifteenth century Salutati, Bruni and the others argued the cause of republican liberty and the life of action, so in the early sixteenth century the ideas of Machiavelli and Guicciardini revolved round the problem of the prince. To that problem we come in the next chapter.

CHAPTER VI

THE RECEPTION OF
THE RENAISSANCE IN ITALY

IN the last chapter I spent most of my time discussing the changing cultural scene at Florence and only touched on other parts of Italy to show that, broadly speaking, the republican background of Florentine civilization was lacking elsewhere. By the end of the fifteenth century Florence had herself more or less fallen into line with the political pattern prevailing in Italy, and had in all but name acquired a prince. Long before that, however, certain parts of Florentine culture had successfully established themselves outside Tuscany. The urban background which, as we have seen, is common to all parts of Italy, facilitated this. With the exception of the pope and the possible exception of the rulers at Naples, the princes of Italy were townsmen and depended on, often actually used, popular support and communal institutions. To the extent that Florentine innovations were civic rather than narrowly republican they could find a ready welcome in other centres, even where there were 'tyrants'.

The 'laicization' (to use an ugly but useful word) of social and moral attitudes accomplished in Florence had an appeal everywhere. The fourteenth-century debate on *otium* and *negotium* had, it is true, encouraged patrons in the princely courts of North Italy to espouse the Petrarchan *otium*; after all they were literally providing the laureate with facilities for writing and research. In the period of hostility between Milan and Florence this princely attitude was a stumbling-block to the adoption of Florentine doctrine, for Giangaleazzo's propagandists continued to advance the argument that letters flourished only under a prince: the debate raged in fact over the rival claims of Roman republic and Augustan empire. But as early as 1402–3 Pier Paolo Vergerio, supporter as he was of the Paduan tyranny of the Carrara, accepted to the full the Florentine doctrine of the active life in his *De ingenuis moribus*;[1] and the same spirit animates the teaching of the two great schoolmasters Guarino and Vittorino. As for the related question of wealth, it needs little imagination to see that the Florentine defence of this would be highly relevant in princely courts, both among princes and courtiers and among the scholars who now in many cases had permanent and honourable employment in their service. Pier Candido Decembrio at the court of Filippo Maria Visconti, Pandolfo Colenuccio at the Este court, Pontano at Naples all advocate the cause of wealth; while at the papal court Lapo da Castiglionchio in 1438 explained Christ's poverty as being merely a temporary position appropriate to conditions in the early empire, while the duty of the pope and the curia in his own day was to acquire possessions and be surrounded with splendour.[2]

The peculiar blend of realism and nobility displayed in the new art at Florence likewise made rapid conquests,

---

[1] Translated by Woodward, *Vittorino*, pp. 96–118; for the date see Baron, *Crisis*, II, 487 n. 20 and refs.

[2] See the excellent discussion of Baron, 'Franciscan Poverty', pp. 26–30.

and one can trace the process in the movement of Florentine artists and architects to other parts of Italy, in the visits —often a turning-point for them—of non-Florentines to the city of Masaccio. This is the side of the Renaissance with which one is, I suppose, most familiar and there is no need to pause over it. Let it be sufficient to recall the effect in northern Italy of Donatello's work in Padua in the decade 1443–53, with all the consequences it had for Mantegna and Bellini, and an ever widening circle of disciples and successors; or of Piero della Francesca's sojourn in Florence in 1439 which was to revolutionize painting in central Italy; of the Brunelleschian church at Castiglione Olona, north of Milan, in the 1440's. It is fair to say that within a century Florentine styles in the building and decorative arts had conquered Italy.

Nor was this advance of the new values merely a veneer. However irritating the skilled humanist official might occasionally be to the grandee not used to expertise in politics,[1] the humanists and artists had a positive role to play in society and government in the princely courts as they had in Florence. The most obvious example of this lies in administration and diplomacy. The humanist chancellor and the humanist ambassador begin to dominate the Italian scene because of the efficacy with which humanists had served the Florentine republic. Pius II recorded in his commentaries the old tradition that Giangaleazzo 'used to say that Coluccio's pen did him more harm than thirty troops of the cavalry of the Florentines'.[2] From then onwards, even if they were

[1] Duke Francesco Maria I (Della Rovere) told Guicciardini 'your business is to confer with pedants', and struck him: J. Dennistoun, *Lives of the Dukes of Urbino*, ed. Hutton, II, 441.   [2] *Commentaries*, p. 165.

figures of small cultural importance, the humanists staffed the chanceries of Italy; they were the new clerks; their documents and speeches conformed to the new style; and many of them (according to Vespasiano da Bisticci) were Florentines.[1] The new style extended far beyond the composition of diplomas and orations.[2] The Florentines had embarked on what one might call 'total diplomacy': the published histories of Bruni and Poggio are part and parcel of their political activity and so it seemed to contemporaries:

Amongst the other exceptional debts which the city of Florence owed to Leonardo and Poggio may be reckoned the following: from the times of the Roman republic onwards there was not to be found any republic or popular state in Italy so famous as was the city of Florence, which had its history written by two authors so illustrious as were Messer Leonardo and Messer Poggio....If the chronicles of the Venetian republic...had been written down and not left unrecorded, the renown of Venice would stand higher than it does today. Likewise the affairs of Galeazzo Maria and Filippo Maria and all the other Visconti would be better known than they are. Every republic ought to set high value upon its writers.[3]

Here again the relevance of Florentine publicism to the courts of Italy is obvious enough: if one could sing the praises of a town, one could exalt a dynasty—and in paint and stone as well as in winged words. The readiness of princes to accept this side of Florentine cultural innovations with both hands has indeed probably been exaggerated. It is clear enough that it neither established despotism nor was essential to sustain despotism: it merely fitted in.

[1] *Lives*, p. 46.
[2] For Italian diplomatic practice in the fifteenth century, see G. Mattingly, *Renaissance Diplomacy*.
[3] Vespasiano da Bisticci, *Lives*, p. 357; cf. p. 366 and Voigt, II, 81.

Such must be one's reflections as one surveys the reception of Renaissance values in Italy, for one should begin not with the great princes but with the little princes. The first clear adoption of humanist assistance in the arts and graces of life and in the day-to-day administrative machine is to be found in the small tyrannies—of the Carrara at Padua, of the Este at Ferrara, of the Gonzaga at Mantua. At Padua we have already encountered Vergerio the schoolmaster, who also wrote the lives of his princely patrons;[1] at Padua during these years there was also an older schoolmaster, Giovanni di Conversino, whose essay 'on the preferable way of life' argues that 'security, prosperity and efficient government' can be found only under the rule of a single man and not in a commune; and only in the ordered progress afforded by a prince can letters truly flourish.[2] This was written when the Carrara were tumbling from power. But Conversino's spirit was carried on in the teaching of two of his pupils—Vittorino da Feltre and Guarino da Verona. Vittorino's school at Mantua, where he was brought by Gianfrancesco Gonzaga, lasted from 1423 to his death in 1446 and its extraordinary qualities—the social mixture of princes and poor men, the humanity with which the humanities were inculcated, the psychological finesse and moral fervour of the master—have made it the most famous school of all time.[3] The Casa Gioiosa could have no real parallels, but Guarino da Verona's school at Ferrara, where he worked from 1429

---

[1] Baron, *Crisis*, I, 108.

[2] *Dragmalogia de eligibili vitae genere*, summarized by Baron, *Crisis*, I, 109–19; there are useful extracts in R. Sabbadini, *Giovanni da Ravenna*, Como 1924, pp. 189–95.

[3] See the excellent essay by Woodward, *Vittorino*, pp. 1–92.

to 1460, was almost as influential as a training ground of princes, administrators and other schoolmasters.[1] It was in Mantua and Ferrara, not in Florence, that humanist educational theory was given practical illustration: we are still directly influenced by the curriculum there established.

It is hardly surprising that it is at Mantua also that one of the first artistic works in the new manner commissioned by a prince is to be seen: the superb frescoes by Mantegna in the Camera degli Sposi in the Castello S. Giorgio, where the Gonzaga family are depicted in all their glory [Plate XVI]. At Ferrara the Palazzo Schifanoia contains the remains of an even bigger pictorial celebration—Cossa's great cycle commemorating Guarino's pupil Borso d'Este. One is almost tempted to suggest that the smaller the court the greater the patronage, the more the resulting works tend to the exaltation of the dynasty: what *great* dynasty dared to construct a monument like the Malatesta temple at Rimini [Plate XIV]? What grander gesture had been made at the time (1455 onwards) than Federico da Montefeltro's palace at Urbino, perched on the rock as a citadel and gallery combined [Plate XV]—the rooms allowing for the men at arms and the library procured from Vespasiano da Bisticci? How superbly Florentine fashions could be taken up elsewhere we can see with the buildings of L. B. Alberti, not only in the Malatesta temple, the Church of S. Francesco at Rimini just mentioned, but at Mantua.[2] In all this one should note that the new classical style in art and architecture was nicely blended by the best masters

---

[1] Woodward, *Education during the Renaissance*, pp. 26–47.

[2] S. Andrea, S. Sebastiano. A good discussion of Alberti's churches in R. Wittkower, *Architectural Principles in an Age of Humanism*, London 1949, pt. ii.

with local elements: this is clearly seen in the painting of Mantegna and later of the Bellini. It is no less true of much of Alberti's building which, it has been well said, sought congruity (*concinnitas*)—for instance in the Rimini temple where the inside of a Gothic building is adapted in this way, though the outside is sheathed in a mask of the new manner.[1] And this congruity was also a Florentine virtue: witness the façade of S. Maria Novella.

Congruity of a very different sort was displayed also in vernacular literature. One of the most interesting developments of the fifteenth century was the emergence, under princely auspices, of the old popular heroic cycles into works of high art. The Carolingian and Arthurian tales had been matter for the vulgar poets of the market-place until Boiardo (d. 1494) wrote his *Orlando innamorato* in the Este court at Ferrara. Ariosto (d. 1533) later on composed his *Orlando furioso* under the same patronage. Later still, and also at Ferrara, came the *Gerusalemme liberata* of Torquato Tasso (d. 1595). These works, which were to be so influential in northern Europe, are a reminder that the literature of an *élite* had its popular background and that the chivalrous North had no monopoly of romantic tales. Even the burlesque *Morgante* of L. Pulci, Florentine in its inventive mockery of the epic, was a product of a princely environment, for Pulci (d. 1484) was an intimate of Lorenzo de' Medici. Nor were these men mere literary lions. Each was employed by his patron in diplomatic and administrative work. The courtier's talents were at different times both an ornament of, and an instrument for, princely government.

[1] Cf. E. Panofsky, *Meaning in the Visual Arts*, New York 1955, pp. 191 ff.

If the smaller courts are so patently interested in bolstering up their prestige and power by patronage of new manners in literature and the arts, this may be partly because in a small principality such gestures are more noticeable.[1] None the less the reception of the Renaissance does seem slower, more erratic, in the greater principalities to which we must now turn: the papacy, Naples, Milan and Savoy.

The popes of the middle ages had employed large numbers of learned men: the popes of the fifteenth century began to employ large numbers of men learned in the humanities; gradually these last begin to determine the general level of culture at the curia, but it is not until the Medicean period of the early sixteenth century that they entirely dominate the papal *entourage*.[2] In all this we should beware of either attributing to individual popes a conscious desire of promoting the new art and literature or of being its enemies. The popes from 1431 to 1549 were intellectual mediocrities, however bright they may have shone as politicians, or as dynasts, or as sinners; mediocrities (that is to say) when compared with Innocent III at one end or Pio Nono at the other.

The very cosmopolitanism of the curia precluded some of the more characteristic features of what one may call the applied humanities from being relevant. No republicanism can be found thriving in a state so absolutely monarchi-

---

[1] Cf. Voigt, I, 532.

[2] The best account, if read with caution, is still Voigt, II, 1–243; this can be supplemented by Pastor, *History of the Popes*, vols. I–XII (down to 1549). V. Zabughin, *Storia del rinascimento cristiano in Italia*, Milan 1924, is a poor thing; the whole matter is still unfortunately bedevilled by confessional prejudice.

cal as the Roman papacy, even it if made a fitful appearance in the city of Rome itself. No patriotism of the kind found at Florence can be transplanted (as it was in Milan, Naples and the lesser courts) to a kingdom where the sovereign changed so often and where no dynasty lent coherence to politics: besides, even if these sorry popes pursued the politics of aggrandizement like their brother princes, they still played lip-service to their headship of an oecumenical church. And certain features of scholarly activity, however much they flourished in the *coulisses* of the Vatican, or the palaces of the cardinals, or the chamber of the pope, were at any rate ostensibly at variance with the teachings of Him whose vicar the pope claimed to be. The bawdy schoolroom humour of Poggio's *Facetiae* was not much more respectable than the *Hermaphroditus* of Antonio Beccadelli (Panormita); what is awkward is that Poggio's book was written while he was a papal secretary and portrays the kind of conversation that delighted the clerks of the curia.[1]

Poggio was in the curia under John XXIII: this reinforces the point that the arrival of humanists there was singularly unplanned; Poggio's reputation as a fruitful scholar is due to another fortuitous circumstance—the deposition of his master at the Council of Constance which deprived him of a job and led to those profitable explorations of monastic libraries which are his chief claim to fame. Back in the curia again in 1423 he was well provided for, and happy in his perambulations of classical monuments in Rome or

[1] I have not seen the *Hermaphroditus*; the *Facetiae* is heavy going and reminds one of the *Cent nouvelles nouvelles*. This humour of bourgeois origin was, of course, to keep its popularity until almost our own day, when it survives, I suppose, only among adolescents of all ages.

in scholarly contacts in Florence when the curia was there for some years after 1434. Leonardo Bruni was also in the curia in these years: so was Antonio Loschi after he left Milan. Gradually men of this stamp saw their numbers increase and their status improve within the hierarchy of the pope's servants. Neither Martin V nor Eugenius IV[1] were much attracted to letters or art and many of the devotees of the humanities merely used the secretariat and other departments of the curia, as they had always done, as stepping-stones to promotion: so Ermolao Barbaro, Piero del Monte, both Venetians, pass upwards through the curia during the pontificate of the Venetian Eugenius IV.

Great importance has always been attached in the history of letters and art to the election as pope of Tommaso Parentucelli, the poor boy who became Nicholas V (1447–55). He had been educated at Florence and Bologna and, after service with Cardinal Albergati and papal diplomatic work, became bishop of Bologna and cardinal. But as pope he was suddenly the master of great wealth and patronage, while his pontificate coincided with a period when the problems facing the papacy were less oppressive than before. His enjoyment of learning was at second hand: but it was enormous. 'Venerare doctos homines, eternitatis vasa—venerare libros, immortalitatis instrumenta', as a contemporary described his programme.[2] The secretaryships in the curia were multiplied for the benefit of scholars; the pope encouraged the translation

---

[1] Eugenius IV's patronage of the school at Bologna and the university at Rome must be remembered in his favour; but this does not signify an interest in the humanities as such.

[2] From the dedication of Nicholas of Lyra by the bishop of Aleria to Sixtus IV in 1471, Voigt, II, 233 n.

into Latin of the principal Greek authors, he attracted to Rome literary and artistic celebrities, he collected books with passion and he embarked on elaborate building in the city.[1] As Voigt pointed out long ago, the men around Nicholas were not of the first rank;[2] the Latin translations of Greek works were very imperfect in many cases and bitter literary feuds rent the chancery. The pope was greedy and possessive over his books, and undiscriminating in his generosity to hungry humanists who, like Filelfo, were not worth supporting. To some of these criticisms there is an answer. In particular Greek scholarship had no Valla and it was, I suppose, not till the eighteenth century that Greek studies approached the refinement and solidity which Latin studies had reached in the fifteenth century.[3] A bitter chauvinism distorted the study of Greek: Poggio could taunt literary enemies by calling them 'semi-Graeculi'; Pius II could take pride in Roman superiority in scholarship and letters;[4] and all this the visiting Greeks often heartily reciprocated, only the saintly Bessarion standing aloof from such petty wrangling. But the up-shot of the pontificate must not be judged solely by its failures, by the projected library which did not emerge, by the abandonment of the scheme for a new St Peter's. For Rome for the first time since classical days was now a

---

[1] For the buildings of Renaissance Rome see the 'Storia di Roma', vol. XXII: F. Castagnoli, Carlo Cecchelli, G. Giovannoni, M. Zocca, *Topografia e urbanistica di Roma*, Bologna 1958.

[2] Voigt, II, 73.

[3] An impression based on J. E. Sandys, *A History of Classical Scholarship*, 3 vols., II (1908): *From the Revival of Learning to the End of the Eighteenth Century*.

[4] Cf. the stimulating and important little book by R. Sabbadini, *Storia del Ciceronianismo*, Turin 1886.

centre of literature, art and scholarship. From now until the early sixteenth century its cultural importance was to rise.

The process was not continuous. Nicholas V's successors Calixtus III (Borgia, 1455–8) and Pius II (Piccolomini, 1458–64) were indifferent to the ambitions of Nicholas. Calixtus was essentially old-fashioned in outlook. Pius was himself a humanist and a prolific writer of *belles-lettres*, yet he had small time to patronize others. The pageantry with which he loved to surround himself gave encouragement to a general taste for display among the princes of the church. Like Nicholas he accepted the desirability of glory, but he reckoned to provide it for himself and not through the support of others. Monuments were likewise intended to secure his lasting reputation, but not in conjunction with Rome. His buildings were erected at Siena, his home town, and at Pienza, the village of his birth which he decorated with a cathedral and other buildings. Of the cathedral's significance for him we may judge from the anathema he laid on anyone who should presume to alter it:[1] there it still stands, a charming monument to Pius II's good taste and irresponsibility. It was in fact under Paul II (Barbo, 1464–71) that a more permanent change occurred in papal attitudes. Despite Platina's sour picture, Paul was an enlightened enough patron.[2] And this trend was confirmed by his successor Sixtus IV (Della Rovere, 1471–84), *restaurator urbis*. At this point the new styles establish themselves firmly in Rome: the Vatican library,

[1] *Commentaries*, pp. 603–4.
[2] Paul's interest in the humanities has recently been freshly examined by R. Weiss, *Un umanista veneziano, Papa Paolo II*, Venice 1957.

the greatest single papal contribution of permanent value to later ages, was established and in 1475 Platina became prefect. And the old Rome of the middle ages, the group of little villages huddled in the ruins of the ancient capital of the world, began to assume its Renaissance form. We are on the way to that identification of art and letters with papal Rome which was accomplished under Leo X and Clement VII. The new cursive hands arrived in the chancery, whence they radiated out to act as models to all Europe.[1] And in the chancery Italian was spoken and no longer Latin.[2] And so firmly was all this established that it coloured the patronage of Alexander VI (Borgia, 1492–1503), the Spanish dynast, and of Julius II (Della Rovere, 1503–13), as we can reflect when wandering through the Vatican or looking down the Via Giulia [Plate XX].[3] The Renaissance in Rome had arrived before the advent of the Medicean popes who brought it to its highest point.

Under Leo X (1513–21) and Clement VII (1523–34) the

[1] Ullman's book on humanist script (above, p. 80) unfortunately does not deal with its diffusion through the papal chancery.

[2] Pastor, I, 242–3 n., gives 1480 as the date when Latin ceased to be obligatory in curial business.

[3] Here is an extract from the *opusculum* dedicated (1510) to Julius II by the Florentine Francesco Albertini, describing ancient and modern Rome: 'Sixtus IV began the restoration of the City.... First he levelled the dark colonnades and then opened up roads and squares, paving the roads. Many churches were reconstructed from their foundations and given again their original form. His successors have emulated him. Finally your holiness has in a short time done more even than Sixtus himself as well as the others. Your buildings indeed justify the truth that this should now be called a New City. In many ways it differs from its ancient predecessor, for how great Rome had once been its very ruins teach us.' Printed at p. 499 of vol. IV (Rome 1953) of *Codice topografico della città di Roma*, ed. R. Valentini and G. Zucchetti ('Fonti per la storia d'Italia'), where literary sources for the history of Rome are collected together for the period of the fourteenth and fifteenth centuries. Vol. III (Rome 1946) covers the twelfth and thirteenth centuries.

Medici produced their first true princes and Rome became
—though in markedly different ways—what Florence had
been a century before, the heart of Italian civilization. This
has been justly characterized by Giuseppe Toffanin as ex-
changing a 'Christian universality' for an 'imperial universality'.[1] Its literary and artistic aspects go hand in hand,
for the prevailing Ciceronianism in Latin (which intensified hatred for eclectic foreign stylists like Erasmus, who
heartily reciprocated this sentiment) is reflected in the art
and architecture of the city; good breeding involved a
manner of writing and a manner of painting;[2] both were
increasingly autocratic. All this nobility had still something of the tensions of its origins in Florence. After all,
its greatest artistic exponent was the Florentine Michelangelo, and some of the groups in the Sistine ceiling and the
whole of the 'Last Judgment' reflect an anguish which is far
removed from the mellifluous poetry and prose of the
Roman writers of the time. But for most writers and artists
the patronage of the popes canalized their productions into
propaganda pieces, however supremely successful. Successful Raphael undoubtedly was: but, even when one has
admitted the beauty of the frescoes in the Vatican or, even
more, some of the devotional paintings [Plate XVIII], one
could wish for other works like the 'Galatea' in the Far-
nesina [Plate XIX], painted for the banker Agostino Chigi
(d. 1520). But Rome was a city of priests and not of
bankers. The painter and the poet were the servants of a
regime that soon had nothing with which to console itself,

[1] *Il cinquecento*, Milan 1945, p. 8; pp. 4–5 stress the important part in
establishing this papal imperialism of Julius II.
[2] H. Wölfflin, *Classic Art* (1898), London 1952, pp. 207–15.

in the world torn asunder by Leo X and Luther, but its cultural ascendancy. Just as Brunelleschi's dome symbolized the Florentine Renaissance,[1] so we may regard as typical of the Roman Renaissance that other gesture—Michelangelo's design for the Capitol [Plate XXI]. The medieval Campidoglio had, like its Roman predecessor, faced the Forum. Now it was turned round and, as we see it today, it faces St Peter's across the streets opened up by Renaissance popes.[2] The forces of communal loyalty in Rome were, like letters and art, to fortify the pope.

These great transformations at Rome from 1471 onwards were accomplished under the leadership of old men of very varying capacities and have a kind of inevitability suggesting that at Rome, as at the smaller courts of Mantua, Ferrara and the rest, patronage of the humanities and the new manner in building and painting was a prop for weak government. This reflection finds support if one briefly reviews the cultural scene in Naples, Milan and Savoy, where great dynasties were established.

At Naples two long reigns, those of Alfonso (sole ruler from 1442 to his death in 1458) and his son Ferrante I (d. 1494), offer at first sight striking evidence of the reception of the Renaissance,[3] for the first earned his title of the

[1] Above, p. 119.

[2] F. Saxl, *Lectures*, 2 vols., London (Warburg Institute 1957), I, 210–14, esp. 208: 'the only secular counterpart to the Borgo Nuovo with the dome of St Peter's'. The actual buildings are nearly all later than Michelangelo, but his design was followed. See the *Topografia e urbanistica di Roma*, pp. 395–8; Francesco Albertini treats the *Palatium conservatorum et senatoris* on the Capitol as a papal palace, *Codice Topografico*, p. 514.

[3] The standard work is E. Gothein, *Die Culturentwicklung Süd-Italiens*, Breslau 1886, pp. 281 ff., supplemented now by the useful book of A. Altamura, *L'umanesimo nel mezzogiorno d'Italia*, Florence 1941.

Magnanimous from the humanists he so lavishly patronized, and the second was almost as generous a supporter of letters as his father. Yet that early symbol of the Renaissance at Naples, the triumphal arch in the Castel Nuovo (1453–67),[1] symbolizes the narrow limits of this interest in the Renaissance, its subordination to the grim realities of feudal power, the two great medieval towers which flank it [Plate XVII]. The Renaissance in Naples was, in fact, fairly superficial and its penetration limited for the most part to the court itself. Alfonso's fame attracted endless dedications, many visitors, but few permanent adherents; only Lorenzo Valla, until he left for Rome in 1448, and Panormita, who made Naples his home, were significant literary figures: and the gay, sociable, wealthy Beccadelli symbolizes the court's attitude to letters under Alfonso, as Pontano symbolizes Ferrante's reign.[2] Both Panormita and Pontano were the centre of literary groups and it has been claimed that the Academy at Naples was the first to to be born, though later than the Florentine and the Roman to be so named.[3] The dynasty certainly profited from the writings of these men. Valla's demolition of the Donation of Constantine and his Life of Ferdinand of Aragon were intended to fortify the king and the first was to have echoes far beyond the mere hostilities of pope and king of Naples.[4] Panormita's *De dictis et de factis Alphonsi regis* (1455) is, of course, the work on which Alfonso's 'magnanimity' chiefly depends. Panormita's protégé Bartolomeo Fazio

[1] Perhaps by F. Laurana.
[2] Gothein, p. 532.
[3] Altamura, p. 28.
[4] Cf. F. Gaeta, *Lorenzo Valla, filologia e storia nell'umanesimo italiano*, Naples 1955.

wrote a history of Alfonso which glorifies his patron, and Pontano exalted Ferrante in a work devoted to the war between the king and John of Calabria.[1] Yet even at the end of the century the Neapolitan humanists seem to provide a grace rather than a necessity; Pontano's charm and pathos have no real relevance to the darkening decline of the dynasty; the tolerant, pastoral values of his circle must be compared with the harsh denunciation of the stories of Masuccio of Salerno, written at this time, where the attack on clerical corruption reminds one that there were social and political problems to which the Neapolitan humanists shut their eyes.[2] The Spanish conquest ended even this: the vernacular remained, but in an anodyne form. It was in this milieu that Sannazzaro's *Arcadia* was born.

The Milanese picture is somewhat different.[3] Giangaleazzo had a few scholars who were prepared to defend his ambitions; his son Filippo Maria (1412–47) was somewhat more energetic in encouraging men of letters; but it was with the new dynasty of Francesco Sforza, who secured the duchy in 1450, that we encounter consistent employment of the new manner in the service of the state and of the family. Just as the cathedral at Milan and the Charterhouse of Pavia continue their Gothic progress only slightly modified by Florentine innovations in the first half

---

[1] For Fazio and Pontano as historians see Fueter, 46–7; cf. *ibid.* p. 48, for Porcellio who deserted his native Naples to write flattering history for Francesco Sforza and G. Piccinino.

[2] Masuccio Salernitano, *Il Novellino*, ed. A. Mauro, Naples 1940: see prologue, pp. 5–6 and the first ten *novelle*.

[3] *Storia di Milano, ubi supra*, VI, 547–608 (E. Garin), VII, 541–97 (E. Garin), 601–746 (E. Arslan on architecture and sculpture), 749 ff. (F. Wittgens on painting).

of the fifteenth century, so the literary scene is dominated as yet by the old-fashioned university at Pavia. Some humanists of distinction were attracted to the court: Panormita and Valla were there in the early 1430's. But the main humanist figure of the reign of Filippo Maria was Pier Candido Decembrio; it is largely through his eyes that we see Milan during these middle years of the century.[1] Decembrio had been, in fact, a servant of the state,[2] but his return to Sforza Milan did not provide the kind of publicist writing which the new duke wanted. At first it seemed as though Francesco Sforza's immortality would be secured, his government reinforced, by the pen of Francesco Filelfo. Filelfo at any rate had no doubt that his *Sforziad* would achieve the former. But this restless, malicious and capable man, who undoubtedly did much for Greek studies in Lombardy, was incapable of the kind of application that a dynast needed. His wanderings were resumed till death caught him in 1481 in the Florence he had had to leave in 1434 for attacking Cosimo. It was in the pages of Bernadino Corio (d. 1519), who was charged in 1485 by Ludovico il Moro to write a history of Milan, that the dynasty really had its effective propagandist. Writing in Italian, at the moment when the Milanese state was to be overthrown, Corio's influence was incomparably greater than that of Francesco Sforza's secretaries Crivelli and Simonetta, or of Filelfo's pupil Merula, who all wrote humanist accounts praising the Sforza and Visconti families.[3] In a sense the artists were a more impressive

[1] Especially in *Vita Philippi Mariae*, chs. LXII–LXIV, RR.II.SS. xx, i, 328–62, with Fossati's commentary. Cf. Garin in *Storia di Milano*, VI, 590 n. 1 for the pendulum of judgments on Milanese culture at this period.

[2] Garin, pp. 604–8; cf. above, p. 140.   [3] Fueter, pp. 49–55.

advertisement of Sforza power and prestige than the writers. If Francesco Sforza's first concern was the great symmetrical *castello*, he also patronized Filarete, whose 'Sforzinda', an ideal town, is a kind of blueprint for princely architecture. And the Milan of Ludovico il Moro is the Milan of Bramante and Leonardo da Vinci, of S. Maria delle Grazie and the 'Last Supper'; it is not irrelevant perhaps to note that Leonardo seems to have derived most benefit not from the humanist writings available to him at Milan, but from the traditional medieval books published there.[1] Here, as in the south, the end of the century brings disaster; Bramante goes to Rome; Leonardo ends his days in France. Charles V is to be master in Milan as in Naples.

The last great court of Italy, Savoy, need not detain us long. Perched in its hills, with manners which for the rest of Italy smacked of transalpine Europe,[2] the duchy was politically dominated by France. It has been neatly said that the Renaissance was smuggled into the towns of this region, so indifferent were the dukes to the appeal of the new literature and the new art.[3] This was not because the princes of Savoy were ignorant of the matter. Had not Aeneas Sylvius Piccolomini been secretary to Amadeus VIII when he became Felix V? Did not Filelfo bestow on Filiberto a moral treatise in 1475, probably in the hope of placing beside the duke his graceless and embarrassing son? There were in the larger centres isolated scholars of some learning in both Latin and Greek literature, and their

[1] Garin in *Storia di Milano*, VII, 596.
[2] Boccaccio and Bandello both reveal this in their *novelle*.
[3] 'Quasi di contrabbando': G. Vinay, *L'umanesimo subalpino nel secolo XV: studi e ricerche*, Turin 1935, p. 9. This is a careful and thorough survey.

general tone as writers and as men compares favourably with the polemics and harum-scarum lives of some other Italian coteries. But the dukes had little use for the new manner; the humanities were 'an exotic fruit...an ornament'.[1]

I began this chapter by deliberately turning my back on Florence, but before leaving the princes and their attitude to new cultural developments we must once again briefly review the Florentine scene. It is a very different Florence from the heroic days of Salutati and Bruni, from the condemnations by Alberti and Bruni of empty learning. Yet even in the heyday of Florentine civic literature one can sense dangers: politically, as we have noted, the city did not really enjoy the kind of liberty which the humanists proclaimed; intellectually there is the danger that this divorce between idea and fact would lead to airy abstraction and to art for art's sake. And this is what happened.[2] 'The victorious princes often protected men of letters: but they made them courtiers',[3] and this loss of liberty must be remembered when we consider Ficino, Politian, Pico and the other great figures of Lorenzo's Florence. Certainly Ficino starts his career under Cosimo—who was influenced by Gemistus Plethon, the one truly paganizing figure of the fifteenth century in Italy[4]—but already under Cosimo one can see the transcendental at work, so to speak, and already in 1463 Ficino had sketched out the ultimate position, the *pia philosophia*, of his later life, the mystery

[1] *Ibid.* p. 241.
[2] Garin, *Umanesimo*, pp. 92–8, 103–45.
[3] *Ibid.* p. 104.
[4] F. Masai, *Pléthon et le platonisme de Mistra*, Paris 1956.

at the heart of reality and its exploration by mystical knowledge of oneself and God. So much for the abstraction. At the other end of the scale is Politian's literary achievement in Latin, Greek and above all in Italian—words of wonder, the grace of language: again a perfection where rhetoric had moved into its own right, detached from life. All of this was, one feels, in sympathy with the painting of Botticelli—sad, diaphanous, serene. And even the contemporary criticism of these developments, whether from Pico della Mirandola or from Savonarola, is transcendental: both proclaiming *concordia*, but with both a peace which is not of this world. We have arrived at the point where one may truly talk of the 'Renaissance Philosophy of Man': but it is Man and not men and women, not the solid bourgeois of Alberti, but a heroic and mythical figure: from Botticelli one moves on to the mature Michelangelo.

Put in this way one might think that the old Florence was a thing entirely of the past. This is not so. For one thing, though Lorenzo did patronize some of the men of letters and some of the artists, his patronage was irregular and probably not very influential.[1] This is in striking contrast to the largely court-engineered humanities and arts of Milan or Naples. Men of genius still flourished at Florence and if they extolled the Medici they did so without much encouragement, as Elizabethans extolled their queen without being paid to do so. Again, however clearly one can see Lorenzo manipulating the state there continued to be variety of opinion, and this went on under the restored Medici of 1512. These are the days of the dis-

A. Chastel, 'La légende médicéene', *Revue d'histoire mod. et contemp.* VI (1959), 161–80.

cussions in the Rucellai gardens[1] where Machiavelli picked up and passed on ideas of liberty, of military discipline, of constitutional reform. In a sense we still have the old antithesis between Italy and Florence, between internal liberty and the larger liberty which will promote internal liberty. But for Machiavelli the condition of general peace is a prince, for Francesco Guicciardini the condition of internal liberty was a ruler, albeit of the discreet Medicean kind.[2] The future lay with the pragmatic Guicciardini, accepting the world as it was and not hoping to master it by *virtù* and rational action,[3] gradually realizing in this way that the new Medici would not, like Cosimo, tolerate the literary fiction of republicanism.[4] Moreover, as the sky of liberty darkened these astonishing Florentines produced an analysis of princely practice which for maturity and subtlety had no parallel. 'Bind the people to the ruler; employ the younger men in service of the ruler; let men forget the responsibilities of government and concentrate on their own pleasure and profit; give men who might be troublesome honour and office and ease.' This is the message of Niccolò Guicciardini, of Lodovico Alamanni, of Francesco Vettori, the architects and servants of the new state: like Salutati their pens are in tune with the world; but the world has changed.[5] At the Bargello one can still see the bust of Brutus, which the last theorist of republicanism Donato Giannotti persuaded Michelangelo

[1] D. Cantimori, 'Rhetoric and Politics in Italian Humanism', *Journ. Warb. and Court. Inst.* I (1937–8), 83–102.

[2] V. de Caprariis, *F. Guicciardini: dalla politica alla storia*, Bari 1950, pp. 51–4.

[3] R. von Albertini, *Das florentinische Staatsbewusstsein*, pp. 241–2.

[4] *Ibid.* pp. 186–7.

[5] See the appendix of documents, *ibid.* and esp. pp. 357, 366–70, 411–12.

to carve for Cardinal Niccolò Ridolfi: the noble head still has the roughness of an unfinished work [Plate XXII]. If one walks upstairs one is confronted with another bust, considerably larger than life: Cellini's portrait of Cosimo I—imperious, remote and dark [Plate XXIII]. It is the difference between Machiavelli and Alamanni, between the past and the future. Elsewhere in Italy the Renaissance has been made the servant of princes and popes. Here at Florence the very world which had bred the civic life and a civic morality to match it had bred also the situation which ended liberty. Michelangelo himself, designing the superb Medici tombs of S. Lorenzo, was preparing the way for Cellini's bust of Cosimo I, for the florid pomposity of the Cappella dei Principi also at S. Lorenzo. The heroic in art could only serve the autocrat in politics.[1]

When the Cappella dei Principi was begun in 1604 Italy had lain for half a century under the yoke of Spain and, as we have seen, Muratori could look back a century after that with satisfaction at the peace which had been thus procured.[2] Such a tranquil acceptance of the end of Italian independence was not possible in the terrible years which followed the French invasion of 1494, and which culminated in the sack of Rome in 1527. For, as never before, the decades round 1500 witness in Italians a consciousness of Italian unity. The best minds of the period are, as it were, compelled to leave the narrow loyalty to city or prince and see the larger loyalty to a country. The old

[1] Cf. G. Weise, 'Il duplice concetto di Rinascimento', *Rivista storica ital.* LXVIII (1956), 5–36, 129–64; esp. 135–46.
[2] Above, p. 41.

dilemma between the liberty of Florence and its survival only in an independent Italy takes on a new and tragic appearance, colouring the writings of Machiavelli and Guicciardini. In them both we see old civic values struggling with the inevitable prince: that redeemer who was to save Italy in the last chapter of Machiavelli's *Prince*; and, in the first pages of Guicciardini's *Storia d'Italia*, that idealized picture of Lorenzo il Magnifico, who maintained adroitly the equilibrium of Italy till his death. For both writers what is at stake is Italy, and, for the first time, Florentine independence is seen in a proper perspective. Guicciardini indeed is aware that the very glories of Italy are a product of that earlier diversity on which I have insisted so much. In his reflections on Machiavelli's *Discorsi* he argues that a united Italy would never have achieved so much: 'una monarchia gli sarebbe stata più infelice che felice'.[1] This, of course, does not mean that the Italian states in fact pursued a national policy: the very opposite is the case, for each prince or town hoped to survive intact by coming to terms with France or Spain.

The cultural unity of Italy was, however, assured. In letters and in art the peninsula shared common styles. The generations of schoolmasters had done their work well. Latin, and a little Greek, was now the bedrock of the educational system: the fire had gone out of the eloquence but the eloquence remained as an educational ideal. And to the ancient classics were now added the Italian classics. The reflections of Machiavelli and Guicciardini are in Tuscan, the language of Dante, Petrarch and Boccaccio which, albeit as a learned language, now begins to dominate every part of

[1] On *Discorsi* I, 12; quoted De Caprariis, *op. cit.* p. 94.

Italy: the greatest sixteenth-century advocate of Tuscan is the Venetian Pietro Bembo (d. 1547), cardinal, courtier, epitome of the last stage of Italian Renaissance letters. Above all there is, within the increasingly rigid foreign control, a uniformity of political practice: it is the age of bureaucracy—hinted at in the Avignon popes, practised to some extent by the Visconti and Sforza in the fifteenth century, triumphant in the Rome of the Medici, in the Milan and Naples of Charles V.[1] With the coming of Cosimo I to power, in this respect too Florence falls into line. Nor did the Reformation disturb this general Italian uniformity: the heretical movements are ruthlessly suppressed,[2] the heretics are exiled or become (what they always tended to be) men of abstract ideas rather than leaders of a mass movement.[3] The imperialism of Leo X, which helped to provoke the reformation in Germany, is to triumph in a baroque religion which had its spiritual affinities with a world of princes. There is, almost literally, no real place in St Peter's for the simple unheroic *pietà* of the young Michelangelo.

In this rapid review of the reception of the Renaissance in Italy I am deeply conscious of many gaps and many questions which need fuller treatment.

Most important of all, perhaps, I have not discussed the economic implications of the cultural changes I have described: until more work has been done to investigate the financing of new buildings and the new directions of

[1] Cf. F. Chabod, 'Y a-t-il un état de la Renaissance?', *Actes du colloque sur la Renaissance* (1956), Paris 1958, pp. 57–74.

[2] F. Chabod, *Per la storia religiosa dello stato di Milano*, Bologna 1938.

[3] Cantimori, *Eretici italiani del cinquecento*, Florence 1939.

general patronage we must remain in the dark as to the relationship of this with broader social trends, themselves often debatable: was the Italian townsman now making more money, or more certain money, from rural property than from commerce? The paintings, the poems, the new churches, the old churches refurbished in the new manner: was this 'investment in culture' all the product of 'hard times' or of an Italian economy pulling out of the four-teenth-century European depression quicker than else-where?[1] Were the Florentine merchants and later the Italian princes laying up treasure in heaven or treasure on earth, as well as contributing to their own power and prestige?

Nor have I had space to discuss how these changes affected the scholars and the scholarship of Italy: I have said hardly anything of the important philosophical developments at Florence, Padua and elsewhere; nor described how the hardening forms of the new principate accorded ill with those littérateurs, such as Filelfo, who inherited from Petrarch a love of liberty and meant by it a desire for irresponsibility and indulgence, or with those artists, like Michelangelo, for whom a patron was, however inescapable, a crippling encumbrance to genius. I have not described the enormous advances of Latin philology, beginning with the epoch-making work of Lorenzo Valla (d. 1457), especially in his *Elegantiae* and his 'Notes on the New Testament'. This was to have important repercussions in both vernacular literature and, through Erasmus, in the field of religion.

The religious field itself also deserves fuller treatment

---

[1] R. S. Lopez, 'Hard Times and Investment in Culture', *The Renaissance, a Symposium*, New York 1952, pp. 19–34.

than the glancing references in previous pages. Late nine-teenth-century scholars treated Renaissance Italy as irreli-gious and paganizing: in our own day the tendency is to point out how many religious paintings were made in comparison with the handful with mythological content, and to assert the piety (however questionable its orthodoxy) of the Florentine academicians, who even took the syste-matic pagan theology of Gemistus Plethon and made it serve the cause of their Christian syncretism,[1] much as Sigismondo Pandolfo Malatesta brought back the Greek's body and placed it in one of the niches of the cathedral at Rimini. Some intellectual detachment from older religious convictions there undoubtedly was. The debate on civic virtue and on the value of the active life could not fail to provoke a fresher awareness of how men behave and its conflict with how men said they ought to behave. Valla was surely right when he said that if the world could vote on the question of pleasure, the Epicureans would win.[2] But even Valla did not concede such a free choice; for less adventurous spirits, including most scholars and artists, the conflict between the senses and the soul continued (as it had for centuries) to be left to the priest to settle. We can surely say of Italians at large what has been said of the Neapolitan humanists: 'Now as before the cult of the Madonna remained the liveliest religious sentiment; reflec-tive enquiry passed her over and the heart held fast to her.'[3] The Madonnas of Raphael and his contemporaries, the *De partu virginis* of Sannazzaro, are at one in this way with

---

[1] Masai, *Pléthon*, pp. 361–2.
[2] *Scritti filosofici e religiosi*, trans. and ed. G. Radetti, 1953, p. 78.
[3] E. Gothein, *Die Culturentwicklung Süd-Italiens*, p. 471.

XIII   THE DUOMO, FLORENCE

XIV   THE MALATESTA TEMPLE, RIMINI

XV   THE DUCAL PALACE, URBINO

XVI MANTEGNA, 'LUDOVICO GONZAGA MEETING HIS SON'

XVII THE TRIUMPHAL ARCH, CASTEL NUOVO, NAPLES

XVIII RAPHAEL, THE SISTINE 'MADONNA'

XIX RAPHAEL, 'GALATEA'

XXI   THE CAMPIDOGLIO, ROME

XXII   MICHELANGELO, 'BRUTUS'

XXIII   CELLINI, 'COSIMO I'

XXIV   SIGNED RENUNCIATION OF PAPAL SUPREMACY, 1534

the devotion of the peasant and the artisan. The fountain of genuine paganism and irreligious sentiment was in any case popular and not learned. Cynicism comes from the street corner, not from the study.

Finally, I have treated these changes as though they left behind no marked regional differences, as though the cultural unification of the peninsula was completely effective. No visitor to Italy needs to be reminded that these still remain and in the Italy of the sixteenth century one great area pursued its way in a fashion markedly at variance with the rest of the country. Venice survived as a republic, and in all sorts of ways stands out as exceptional: her solemn, grand buildings have the kind of magnificent simplicity which was drowned elsewhere in baroque; her painters have a sensuousness and vitality which for long refuted the abstract nobility of Renaissance Rome. Venice all through the fifteenth century acts like the United Provinces in the seventeenth century, a refuge for all manner of expatriates, and in the sixteenth stands, the envy of the Italian utopians, *ben governato*, a rock of republican liberty, where Veronese could stand up to the inquisition to defend his 'Feast in the House of Levi',[1] of which Aretino could write 'O patria universale! o libertà comune! o albergo de le genti disperse! quanti sarebbero i guai d'Italia maggiori, se la tua bontà fusse minore!'[2] In all this there is a distinct flavour of Florence, the Florence of the early fifteenth century with its identification of culture and political liberty, just as there is a parallel

---

[1] Accademia, Venice.
[2] See the whole letter, I, 20 (1530) in *Lettere*, ed. S. Ortolani, Turin 1945, pp. 13–15; cf. *La cortigiana*, III, vii.

in the conscious efforts made by Venice in the foreign-dominated Italy of the 1530's and 1540's to act, as Florence had done faced with the Visconti, as the defender of Italian values. The linguistic development of the Republic of St Mark offers remarkable testimony to the penetration of Tuscan literature. Not only was the warmest champion of Tuscan the Venetian Bembo, as we have seen, but the earlier progress of the language resulted in the *dialect* of Venice becoming nearer to Florentine than any other in Italy. Thus transplanted, something of Florentine civic humanism continues to flourish in Venice throughout the sixteenth century.[1] It is, however, not until the nineteenth century that Venice truly belongs to Italy. This should remind us that, while the Renaissance first gave Italy a vivid picture of unity and a culture which continued to act as a unifying force, the country had to wait for three centuries for this to become a political reality.

[1] Cf. now the paper by H. G. Koenigsberger, which I had not seen when the above was written: 'Decadence or Shift? Changes in the civilization of Italy and Europe in the sixteenth and seventeenth centuries', *Trans. R. Hist. Soc.* ser. 5, x (1960), 1–18, esp. 9–13.

CHAPTER VII

THE RECEPTION OF
THE RENAISSANCE IN THE NORTH

I COME finally, and with far too little space at my disposal, to the reception of the Renaissance outside Italy. What had Italy to offer as a result of the cultural changes I have spoken of? She had produced a defence of the active life and of the virtue of possessions as against the old ideal of renunciation. She had made education in classical Latin the basis of this new civic morality. She had thus demonstrated the value of classical studies and, parallel with this, the enormous advantages of a single literary language fixed in orthography, firm in grammar, rich in forms—all of which was exemplified in the vernacular as well as in Latin. And in art she had developed styles which in their naturalism and nobility gave a picture of the world in accord with the new moral attitudes. The decisive steps in each of these achievements had been made in Florence in the first half of the fifteenth century.

At first sight all these new attitudes might seem to have been immediately acceptable in the North. The moral problem was no different in Germany, France or England than in Italy. There, too, there was practical enjoyment of the good things of life, practical involvement in family and public affairs, great social insistence on *largesse*, and the contrasting ideal of the monastery. It is admittedly the case that the wealth of Italy was for long relatively greater than the wealth—dispersed, mainly agrarian—of northern countries, and it had come to Italy sooner: in matters of comfort and convenience, Milan and Florence were more advanced by 1300 than any town of France or England, let alone the draughty castles where the magnates spent most of their time. But this apart—and it is a question of degree only—the harsh conflict between what men did and what they were told, however perfunctorily, they ought to do is as marked out of Italy as in it. One aspect of this is the pervading anti-clericalism of all popular literature: less savage than the Italian sentiment, but present all the same. Another aspect is the progressive irrelevance of traditional education. After all it was at Paris and Oxford that Nominalism took root first, and as it became fashionable this philosophy of northern doctors could not have been more remote from the needs of the day. As a result we see the men of law coming to the fore in the North, as they had done for different reasons in Italy, and in England even developing in the Inns of Court a completely new kind of higher education divorced from the university altogether. The men who got on in France and England on the basis of letters were increasingly men of law—civilians on the Continent, mainly common lawyers in England; the day of the all-triumphant doctor of theology was passing. Everywhere schools were springing up to teach the sons of gentlemen and burgesses; in so far as these young men went to universities, they went for arts and they treated the ancient corporations as finishing schools.

Linguistic difficulties were found in the North as well as in Italy: there was no agreed German, or French, or English as yet, and the position in the Spanish peninsula was even worse. In France and England the existence of a semi-permanent centre of administration in Paris and London was exercising a steady influence in favour of one variety of French and English, but French and English prose were clumsy and inchoate even by the end of the fourteenth century, ready (if one may put it this way) to be instructed by a language more disciplined than clerk's Latin. With literacy rising a more streamlined vernacular was increasingly desirable.

As for literature, art and architecture, the last was in the North pursuing its own way—ecclesiastical buildings developing ever more decorated styles of Gothic and in England proceeding farther into the rich solemnity of Perpendicular. This late Gothic, while in its French and German forms it had much to offer Italy and was, as we have seen, influential in North Italy, had no need to seek inspiration elsewhere. In painting, too, the later middle ages see Gothic influence in Italy, while in Flanders and north France a realist school developed, within a framework of Gothic arrangement, which at an astonishing number of points parallels and indeed anticipates contemporary trends in Italy. It has indeed been claimed that fourteenth- and fifteenth-century Europe is at one in its realism[1]—and that this is true also of literature: the second part of the *Roman de la Rose* and Chaucer are called as witnesses. The influence in painting in the fifteenth century was rather from the north to the south: Fazio in his book on famous men included four painters only: and of these two were Jan van Eyck and Roger van der Weyden, the former being described as 'nostri saeculi pictorum princeps'. The

[1] By G. Weise, 'Duplice concetto'.

Italians saw much that was congenial to them in the Flemish style—an exhilarating naturalism, a piety more moving than the native kind, and a technical superiority: Vasari attributed the discovery of oil as a medium to Jan van Eyck.[1] The Flemish and North French masters did not know the rules of perspective, but in practice they had achieved an astonishing capacity for painting as if they did know them, and in one field—the portrait—the French were ahead of the Italians. In brief, the style and content of northern literature and northern art are pursuing developments strikingly similar to those in the Italy of the fourteenth and fifteenth centuries.

Finally, in the field of government and administration northern princes had little to learn. What could old Archbishop Ottone Visconti teach an Edward I or a Philip the Fair about getting cash or managing men? Not very much, I think. But the Italians were quicker off the mark in some of the techniques of administration—picking them up from Avignon or from mercantile practice more readily than the French, or the English or the Germans. We meet the new secretaries, the new diplomatic agents in Italy before we find them ousting the old officers in the North.[2] But the need for all these Italian devices is evident in the North, at any rate episodically, from the end of the thirteenth century onwards. It was not an accident that Burgundy in the mid-fifteenth century produced a Philippe

[1] I paraphrase here E. Panofsky, *Early Netherlandish Painting*, 2 vols., Cambridge, Mass. 1953, pp. 1–2; R. Weiss, 'J. van Eyck and the Italians', *Italian Studies*, XI (1956), 1–15, XII (1957), 7–21.

[2] Cf. Mattingly, *Renaissance Diplomacy*; F. L. Ganshof, *Histoire des relations internationales*, I. *Le moyen âge*, Paris 1953, pp. 263–302, gives a good picture of the situation in the north of Europe.

Commynes for Louis XI: less literate but hardly less effective servants of the French crown had been in continuous action since the time of his predecessor Pierre Flotte. Equally, a gentry ready to serve the crown could be fitted for that service by the grammar school or the *lycée* better than by the parson and a year at Oxford.

In all these ways the northern scene in the later middle ages seems ripe for the adoption of the new attitudes and the new manners. Why do they not begin to be really influential outside Italy until the sixteenth century? Any answer to this question must remain tentative, for no adequate survey of the Renaissance north of the Alps has yet been made and such studies as have been undertaken are on the whole not backed by the necessary knowledge of Italian history and Italian culture.[1] It seems clear, nevertheless, that the problem is likely to be solved by examining the structure of northern society and noting points where it differs significantly from that found in Italy.

Much learning has been devoted to describing the travellers who went from the North to Italy in the later middle ages, though most of them tell us little enough of what they thought of it. Even more interesting would be a thorough investigation of the Italians who saw the North.[2] One or two of them were pretty communicative

[1] But there is a good survey of this situation in the field of scholarship in R. Weiss's chapter in the *New Cambridge Modern History*, I, 95–126.

[2] A word of illustration from the English side may be useful. Apart from letters by visitors (of which an indication can be gained from R. Weiss's book referred to below, p. 188), a certain amount of information is provided by Pius II in his *Commentaries* and in the *Europa*; in about 1483 Dominic Mancini included a description of England in his *Usurpation of Richard III*, ed. C. A. J. Armstrong, Oxford 1936; the *Italian Relation*, Camden Society,

and from their amused and sometimes superior attitudes some of the barriers between Renaissance Italy and the as yet unresponsive North can be discerned. They found it a land of castles not towns, where women were freer and kings more powerful than at home. The great men of the North were landed magnates who were only just becoming familiar with the gravitational pull of the court and the capital city. Even kings were most at home in their hunting lodges, which, like those of nobles, were more comfortable now, but still mounted the crenellation of an earlier age, symbol as it was of military magnificence.[1] The king, ruling a large country, with much larger revenues than the princes of Italy, had an authority which by the fourteenth century in France and England had made him the focus of patriotic loyalty, and enabled him (so Italians sometimes thought) to be more brutal and luxurious than was possible in Italy where there were no accepted traditions of royal wilfulness.[2] Strong monarchy at the centre, a style of life determined in the main by a predominantly rural nobility, these are sharp differences from the regionalism and bourgeois values of Italy. The northern ethos had a kind of natural hostility to Italian urban life: the sharp distaste of the German aristocrat Otto of Freising in the twelfth century to the Italian commune has its echoes still in the early sixteenth when Lemaire de Belges

London 1847, ed. Charlotte A. Sneyd, is dated about 1500. From then onwards Italian diplomatic reports become fuller and more frequent, and can be supplemented by other sources, such as Bandello. What we need is a book like G. Ascoli's *Grande Bretagne devant l'opinion française* dealing with Italian opinion.

[1] Cf. F. Gibelin, *Les Châteaux de la Loire*, Paris 1957.

[2] M. Bandello, *Tutte le opere*, ed. F. Flora, Milan 1934–5, 2 vols., I, 1054–5 (England), II, 650 (Guelders), 655 (Burgundy), 701 (Spain).

writes with suspicion of the republicans at Venice.[1] Finally, the tensions of a moral kind which undoubtedly existed in the North were there both less obtrusive (partly no doubt because of the slower urban development) and better contained within the framework of traditional teaching. The heresiarchs Wyclif and Hus are, in their completely antithetical ways, both very conservative figures. No doubt a rumbling underground social and religious dissatisfaction produces in the North a millenarian radicalism which has some striking parallels with Joachimism and other forms of popular prophecy in Italy, but it was not, as Professor Cohn has shown,[2] very significant in France and it does not influence England till the seventeenth century. It is also of some interest to note that the old abnegation, the old austerities were in the North throwing up lively forms, in which mysticism was contained very reasonably in institutional forms: I refer to the religious movements of the Rhineland and the Low Countries, and above all to the Brethren of the Common Life. The *ars moriendi* literature of the later middle ages has its beginning in northern Europe, not Italy; in Italy in popular iconography we have the Triumph of Death, in northern Europe we have the Dance of Death, where the individual in society meets his fate class by class.[3]

Now the cultural developments in Italy had, as we have seen, three stages: a period in the fourteenth century, culminating about 1370, in which a few isolated figures of genius, of whom Petrarch is the greatest, speculated

---

[1] *Illustrations de Gaule*, ed. Stécher, I, 7.
[2] N. Cohn, *The Pursuit of the Millennium*, London 1957.
[3] See the interesting study by Alberto Tenenti, *Il senso della morte e l'amore della vita nel Rinascimento*, Turin 1957, esp. pp. 91 ff., 430–61.

afresh on the moral and literary problems that faced them; this is followed by nearly a century when the leaders in ideas and art are the Florentines, a period of civic literature when the study of the humanities was at the service of the republic; and finally we come to the century from about 1450 to 1550 when Renaissance styles in morality and art are adopted by the courts of Italy and with the greatest ostentation by the court of Rome. Granted the existence in the North of a situation in which the Italian innovations were inherently relevant, and of social and ideological impediments to their reception, how did the contacts between Italy and the North proceed in each of these periods? Space, my own lack of knowledge and the absence of satisfactory studies of the northern Renaissance must limit an examination of this to the cases of France and England.

The first Renaissance age, that of Petrarch and Boccaccio, should, one might guess, have been afforded particularly ready appreciation in France. Petrarch spent much time in Avignon, where the popes were French, where naturalistic art flourished. Petrarch was in direct contact with several French scholars, and secured for himself an invitation to be laureated at Paris, which he later visited. But these seeds bore no fruit. The poet's assertion of Italian superiority, in letters to French friends, was only one barrier to the reception of his influence. More important, the French scholars with whom Petrarch was in correspondence were unable to understand his real originality: it was the traditional moralist of the *De remediis utriusque fortunae* who was admired in the fourteenth and fifteenth centuries: not the critic of traditional philosophy, not the introspective, not the epic poet.[1] It was to Rome that Petrarch went for his crown, and this turning of his back on the northern world was on the whole reciprocated—especially by the courtiers and clerks who argued that the pope should stay in Avignon and resented the charge of barbarism. Equally insignificant is Chaucer's contact with Italy. The French influence in his work is profound; but what came of the meeting with Petrarch (if it took place) or of his reading of Boccaccio? Surely it is important that such debt as Chaucer had to Boccaccio is to be seen in his 'Palamon and Arcite' (the *Knight's Tale*) and in *Troilus and Criseyde*: it was in short the courtly side of Boccaccio that interested Chaucer, not the bourgeois of the *Decameron*, still less the scholar of the Latin works.

During the second stage the cultural contacts between Italy and the North were encouraged by the great Councils of the church. Especially at Constance (1414–18) the intellectuals were brought together. But while Poggio and others embarked at this stage on a period of wandering in the North, from which resulted the discovery of some classical texts, the real message of Salutati, Bruni and the rest was so clearly rooted in Florentine patriotism, so markedly civic in tone, that it comes as no surprise that it was not apprehended in France or England. A new interest in grandiloquence, especially in vernacular and Latin prose, is certainly found at this time: it is the age of the *rhéto-riqueurs* in Burgundy,[2] of Abbot Whetamstede and his

---

[1] An important essay by Franco Simone, 'Sur quelques rapports entre humanisme italien et humanisme français', *Pensée humaniste et tradition chrétienne* (Colloques... du centre int. de la recherche scientifique), Paris 1950, pp. 241–77.

[2] G. Doutrepont, *La Littérature française à la cour des ducs de Bourgogne*, Paris 1909.

'verborum florida venustas'.[1] But the art and literature of the North were—even in the case of the Flemish painters—securely sealed in courtly circles.[2] It is surely significant that in England the two men who took the liveliest interest in Italian literary developments were magnates.[3] Humphrey duke of Gloucester, and John Tiptoft earl of Worcester, who both figure as customers and as patrons in Vespasiano da Bisticci's *Lives*, are miniature Italian princes; they evoke not Florence, but Urbino and Mantua and Ferrara; they anticipate the third stage in the Italian Renaissance, when it had left the commune for the court.

The really decisive moment in the reception of humanist values comes with the end of the fifteenth century and the early decades of the sixteenth. The essential condition for the North's comprehension of Italian innovations was that these should be in a form immediately intelligible to a society which in the main was princely and aristocratic. This, as we have seen, had been accomplished during the late fifteenth century in Italy. The Renaissance, in its art and in its literature, was urban in origin; and so for the most part were the dynasties of Italy; but dynasties they were and with the prince dominant in Italy, with the courtier and the bureaucrat, the Italian scene was not so

---

[1] E. F. Jacob, 'Verborum florida venustas', *Essays in the Conciliar Epoch*, 2nd ed., Manchester 1953, pp. 185–206.

[2] H. Baron's chapter in the *New Cambridge Modern History*, I (1957), pp. 50–75, is the best general survey of the fifteenth century in the North from the cultural point of view.

[3] On developments in fifteenth-century England see the fundamental work of R. Weiss, *Humanism in England during the Fifteenth Century*, 2nd ed., Oxford 1957; a good survey of the literature on the French side, in default of an adequate study, is provided by R. Bossuat, *Manuel bibliographique de la littérature française du moyen âge*, Melun 1951, part ii, ch. XIII, 'L'humanisme en France', pp. 578–86.

dissimilar from that in northern Europe. The scholars and painters were for the most part not now to be found defending or illustrating a bourgeois way of life: they were in Rome or Milan in the *entourage* of a pope or a duke, mingling with his other dependants. The ambassadors and scholars and gentlemen who travelled south over the Alps were more at home than they had been a century before.

This seems to me to be the real explanation for the sudden but undoubted accessibility of Italian values at the start of the sixteenth century. To it should, perhaps, be added one further feature—the development at Florence, home of the humanities, of religious attitudes more consonant with northern sentiments than the civic principles of the age of Salutati and Bruni. It has been argued[1] that when Colet and Lefèvre d'Étaples visited Italy they were both in tune with, and inspired by, the city of Ficino and Pico. The deep religious mood of Neo-Platonist ideas at this stage imbued such visitors with a fresh reverence for Latin language and literature, for Greek and the Greek philosophers both pagan and Christian, as means to the Christian life. The *devotio moderna* of the North could thus link up with the *devotio moderna* of the Florentine Academy. There is undoubtedly truth in this, but it must not be pressed too far, for two reasons. First, an even more potent influence on northern religion was to be Erasmus's discovery of Valla's *Adnotationes* on the New Testament: there was nothing very Florentine or in a sense religious in Valla; but from this was to flow the Erasmian attitude to the Scriptures, the translation of the Gospels, and much else. Second, if for a couple of decades Florence offered

[1] Baron, *New Cambridge Modern History*, I, 63–6.

religious inspiration to fortify and excite northern scholarship, autocratic Catholicism at Rome for an even longer period made devout men view askance many of the developments in art and letters which we have been considering. I am not here referring only to the shocked horror which the corruption and splendour of Rome produced in pious visitors, as they did in Luther: this is an old story, as we can see from the novel of Boccaccio about the converted Jew.[1] I am referring to the huge gesture of St Peter's, to the Ciceronianism of Medicean Rome which Erasmus attacked in his *Ciceronianus*, to the monstrous lack of even the appearance of charity in the popes from Pius II to Clement VII. In so far as the popes had captured the leadership of Italian *belles-lettres* and art by the end of the fifteenth century, and to a large extent they had, this offered a religious discouragement to the transmission to the North of new ideas and techniques. The curia had not been admired north of the Alps for centuries. Now its arrogant literary and artistic monopoly was a further irritation. All this lasted far longer than the brief period of Florentine religious fervour. The discouragement of northerners by Italian religion in this kind of association with literature and the arts was a deadly blow at any understanding built on the flimsy foundations of Florentine Platonism.

However ready Italy and the North were for the exchange of new ideas, means had to be found for their transmission and for their establishment in a new environment. The transmission of the Italian ideas seems to have taken

[1] *Decameron*, I, ii.

three main ways: the Italian scholar and artist in the North; the northern visitor to Italy; and the circulation of books and works of art. As for the establishment of the humanities as a permanent feature of culture, we need only consider education.

The diaspora of Italian humanists was sometimes explained at the time by the wars in Italy; thus Polydore Vergil accounted for it, writing immediately after the sack of Rome.[1] But one suspects that pressures—economic, moral and cultural—were to some extent operating before 1494. Poggio, in search of employment after 1415, came to England for a brief time; both he and Filelfo considered settling in France, where Petrarch had been tolerably well provided for; and Pier Paolo Vergerio ended his life in obscurity in Hungary. These are all considerable figures: many lesser men found employment north of the Alps.[2] The most influential of these Italians in the fifteenth century was Aeneas Sylvius Piccolomini, who passed from the service of Felix V to that of Frederick III in 1442. The future Pope Pius's experiences in the Austrian chancery were not happy, as we can see from his correspondence at this time:

Literature flourishes in Italy [he wrote in 1444] and princes there are not ashamed to listen to, and themselves to know, poetry. But in Germany princes pay more attention to horses and dogs than to poets—and thus neglecting the arts they die unremembered like their own beasts.[3]

[1] *Anglica Historia*, ed. Hay, Camden Series, London 1950, p. 145 collation.
[2] Cf. Weiss, *Humanism in England*, for Italians in fifteenth-century England.
[3] *Der Briefwechsel der Eneas Silvius Piccolomini*, ed. Wolkan (Fontes Rerum Austriacarum), I, i, 329–30; on Aeneas as the apostle of humanism in Germany see Voigt, *Aeneas Sylvius Piccolomini als Papst Pius II*, 3 vols., Berlin 1856–63, II, 342 ff.; and on humanism in Germany in general, *Wiederbelebung*, II, 261–315.

In fact Germany in the second half of the fifteenth century seems to have been more responsive to Italy than either France or England: not only the odd aristocrat (like the Count Palatine Frederick I) but a few patricians and others from Augsburg and Nürnberg looked to Italy for a new educational and literary programme. By the end of the fifteenth century and early years of the sixteenth a patriotic urge combined these scattered efforts into an impressive cultural movement which was deflected by the Reformation.

It is necessary to note that these fifteenth-century scholars were selling themselves abroad, so to speak: Poggio and Aeneas Sylvius were anxious for employment and found it hard to get. By the end of the century much less impressive figures found it much easier to get posts and preferment in France and England. Here England is, in a way, a better case than France—for both before 1494 and after there were many political refugees in and around the French court as a result of French concern with Italian affairs; and in the train of the retreating French armies came scholars and artists who might not otherwise have lived in France.[1] Early Tudor England[2] was involved in all this somewhat distantly, and we must trace the visitors

[1] No really good general account of Franco-Italian cultural contacts exists, but there are some excellent partial studies. The best general survey remains A. Tilley, *The Literature of the French Renaissance*, 2 vols., Cambridge 1904. A very attractive anthology of extracts with a useful commentary is P. Villey, *Les Sources d'idées au XVIe siècle*, Paris 1912; cf. also F. Simone, *La coscienza della Rinascita negli umanisti francesi*, Rome 1949.

[2] There is no adequate history of the Renaissance in England in the sixteenth century. The book by L. Einstein, *The Italian Renaissance in England*, New York 1902, is not reliable but has not been replaced. On the purely literary side there is now, however, the exciting volume in the 'Oxford History of English Literature' by C. S. Lewis, *English Literature in the Sixteenth Century excluding Drama*, Oxford 1954.

to other occasions than war. The papal officials and envoys of the late fifteenth century were men trained in the new respect for the humanities: the brothers Gigli, Adriano Castelli, Polydore Vergil were only a few of the humanists who were collectors or sub-collectors of Peter's Pence and who acted as papal agents in England: all were well rewarded in ecclesiastical preferment by the crown, and Polydore Vergil spent most of his working life in England, one of the most influential lesser literary figures of the early sixteenth century. Other scholars there were in plenty who came to England in order to make a career: Andrea Ammonio, who became Latin secretary to Henry VIII, Silvestro Dario and Peter Vannes who were employed as diplomatic agents; and later still the soldiers, the military engineers and the men of science. There can be no doubt that the crown had a use for the humanist in the early sixteenth century which had not existed in the fifteenth. It is not merely that a new dynasty found it convenient to encourage Vergil to write his *Anglica Historia* as a defence of the regime: even if there had not been a revolution in 1485 there would have been a positive advantage in a laudatory account of England from a man trained in the new style.[1] Likewise when diplomacy was conducted by orators who had studied Cicero and Quintilian it was useful to have men like Ammonio to write despatches: kings and great men had need, as never before, of active, educated and sharp-witted young men like Bandello's secretary, 'assai dottrinato e bellissimo scrittore e uomo intromettente ed avvenevole',[2] who could reply

[1] For Vergil and his history see my *Polydore Vergil*, Oxford 1952.
[2] Bandello, *Tutte le opere*, I, 528.

in suitable Latin and with the same beautifully clear hand-writing to the Italian documents now entering the country in large numbers. Better still if there were natives to fill the bill—like Richard Pace and Thomas More. All of this could equally well have been illustrated from France, for before 1494 we see Paolo Emilio of Verona engaged there on his historical work, much as Vergil in England,[1] but with no dynastic catastrophe to explain royal support of his work. France had certainly a fuller and earlier contact with High Renaissance art than England: Leonardo and later on Cellini were in France; Torrigiano, whose claim to fame was that as a young man he had broken Michelangelo's nose, was the only significant Italian artist in early Tudor England. But in a sense it was through Germany and above all through Dürer that all the northern world learned to appreciate Italian art; the reception was a slow business, much slower than the reception of letters.[2]

The second method of transmission of Italian values is the northern visitor to Italy. Here again the French evidence is overwhelming, but distorted by war and diplomacy. The slenderer but more normal contacts of England have a corresponding significance.[3] Many clerks continued to frequent the Roman curia down to the break with Rome; a very active diplomacy took men to the Italian courts; and, with a thirst which could not be

---

[1] For Paolo Emilio see Miss K. Davies's Ph.D. thesis, Edinburgh University, 1953.

[2] Cf. Panofsky, *Meaning in the Visual Arts*, pp. 276–80.

[3] Down to 1525 see George B. Parks, *The English Traveler in Italy*, 1. *The Middle Ages*, Rome 1954; Clare Howard, *English Travellers of the Renaissance*, London 1914, is mainly concerned with the Elizabethan traveller.

satisfied at home, scholars sought the land of Latin eloquence. Colet, Linacre, Lily, Pole—the list of serious students is a long one. And the list of students who were not serious would be much longer. Thomas, in his *History of Italy* (1549) remarks on the number of foreigners in the country, 'specially of gentlemen, whose resort thither is principally under pretence of study'.[1] Nor were the busy Tudor bureaucrats unaware of the need to tap this source of talent, as we can see from Mr Zeeveld's study of the households maintained in Italy at the expense of Wolsey and Henry VIII—whence came some of the apologists of Tudor policies.[2] An indication of the progress made by these Anglo-Italian contacts is provided by that remarkable document: the signed renunciation of papal headship of the church in England, 1534.[3] There are 104 signatures of clerks, from the two archbishops down to humble proctors; and of these no fewer than eighteen sign their names in humanist script.[4] If we subtract the name of the Italian Peter Vannes, we are left with seventeen men who had been touched with the new style [Plate XXIV]. I do not wish to exaggerate the point; they were by no means a fair sample of the whole body of clergy. But that so sizeable a number of important clergy knew something of the italic manner as early as the mid fifteen-thirties is a clear indication of the spread of Italian influence: it is ironical that our evidence comes from a document in which England was breaking from Rome.

[1] Quoted Einstein, p. 119; see *ibid*. Hoby's (1549) remark on the large numbers of Englishmen in every Italian city.
[2] W. Gordon Zeeveld, *Foundations of Tudor Policy*, Cambridge, Mass. 1948.
[3] B.M. Add. MS. 38656. Plate XXIV shows only the first leaf.
[4] There are 105 signatures, but Roland Lee signs twice.

The third way in which ideas and attitudes came from Italy was in print: I say in print because I wish to include engraved pictures whose influence on northern artists was obviously great—though I believe we do not yet know enough about it properly to evaluate it. As for the printed book, this was, as Voigt proudly pointed out, Germany's contribution to the Renaissance.[1] Printing as such is, however, beside the point: the books printed were in the North what the North had long read—the old romances, the Bible, the service and school books. But granted a public for the new Italian values, these could spread quickly by the new medium. This is very clearly seen in the field of learned works, where the Italian printers early established their leadership: Aldus Manutius at Venice is the great example of this. It was Aldus who first used italic type in 1501, thus giving wide diffusion to the humanist hand, examples of which were, of course, to be found entering northern Europe as soon as it was used in books and despatches. Roman type (used in Italy in a perfected form in the 1470's) and italic quickly began that career of conquest which was to subjugate the northern gothic or black letter: England had virtually capitulated by the 1580's and only Germany resisted with success. In France, Spain and Switzerland the new type faces were dominant by the early decades of the sixteenth century.

The moral innovations, the most serious contribution of the humanist to the anxieties of the day, could also come in print by way of prefaces extolling Cicero and the active life, praising oratory and the service of the community and the prince. Beyond that the Italians had theorists at work

[1] *Wiederbelebung*, II, 311.

who were particularly adapted to instruct the northern world in the Renaissance attitude to politics. Here I am emphatically not thinking of Machiavelli. Earlier I posed the rhetorical question: what could the Visconti teach kings like Edward I or Philip the Fair? Now let me ask: What could Machiavelli teach Commynes or Thomas Cromwell? The book I *am* thinking of is Baldesar Castiglione's *Courtier*, drafted in 1508 and printed in 1528.

This work, and others like it, exactly expressed what was most easily assimilated by the northern world in the latter-day Renaissance in Italy. Its dignity and mannered elegance, its respect for both martial accomplishments and literary attainments, its placing of talent at the service of a prince, all expressed Italian civility in a way perfectly attuned to the aristocratic North. Long before the book was translated into English by Thomas Hoby in 1561 it was exercising its influence in works like Sir Thomas Elyot's *Gouernour*.[1] It was from books like this (sometimes read in Latin, often read in Italian once the language began to be widely known in the second half of the sixteenth century) that the squirearchy gradually adopted the new morality.[2] Chivalry had paved the way for this: let us remember that Castiglione came to England to receive the Garter for his master, the duke of Urbino.

Much the same is true of France. Here again the literature of courtesy had a very wide diffusion: François de Belleforest translated Giovanni della Casa's *Galateo*;

[1] *The Boke named The Gouernour*, London 1531. There were seven further editions by 1580.

[2] E.g. *The Courtier* of 1561 is reprinted in English in 1577, 1603; in 1588 it appeared in parallel columns of English, French and Italian: Latin versions were published in 1571, 1577, 1585, 1593, 1603, 1611.

Castiglione's *Courtier* was twice translated, by Jacques Colin and by Gabriel Chapuys. All of these books were popular and encouraged a large French literature of like purpose. In any case the printers of Lyons and Paris were eager transmitters of Italian books and ideas, as we can see from the literature assimilated by Rabelais and Montaigne, both of whom—like so many of the writers of sixteenth-century France—knew Italy also at first hand. For those who were not able to travel there were Italian courtiers in France itself, and not least the remarkable bishop of Agen, the Dominican Matteo Bandello (1485–1561). Bandello's *Novelle* exactly reflect the courtly humanities, the graceful groups of well-bred gentlemen whose lives are passed in agreeable conversation and who regale themselves with tales of wit and of amorous intrigue: his *novelle*, as he says himself, are both gossipy trifles and true: 'le mie ciancie… non sono favole ma vere istorie'.[1] The king and his subjects, the king and his courtiers were no new phenomenon in France and England. The Italians provided them with a reasoned philosophy of service and a delight in the rewards of activity and expensive leisure.

All of this needed to be consolidated in an educational reform; and was so consolidated in the course of the sixteenth century. In this we must, I believe, hesitate to picture a wholesale conversion of existing institutions to new disciplines, or a wholesale creation of new schools. In Italy we have at first to trace the descent of *literae humaniores* from schoolmaster to schoolmaster: the pupils of Giovanni di Conversino, the pupils of Barzizza, of

[1] *Tutte le opere*, I, 659, 778.

Vittorino, of Guarino: each time there are more pebbles thrown into the water, the circles of ripples grow wider, until the whole lake of Italian learning is astir. And so it is in England, France and elsewhere on this side of the Alps. And we should note that the surface of northern learning had already been ruffled before the sixteenth century: Erasmus encountered the humanities at Deventer—long before he went to Paris and met Gaguin and the Italians there: he was contemptuous of his earlier training, but it was nevertheless a long way from the sort of school he would have attended two centuries earlier; in Germany there was Ludwig von Dringenberg's school at Schlettstadt; in England there was the Oxford schoolmaster whose *vulgaria* have just been published;[1] St Antony's school in London did not exactly dim the genius of Thomas More; and so we say also of the Oxford of Colet. Polydore Vergil's account of the reception of good letters is worth noting. He attributes it to prelates and a noblewoman and begins with the Lady Margaret who, at the suggestion of Bishop Fisher, founded Christ's College and St John's College at Cambridge; Bishop Alcock founded Jesus; William Smith, bishop of Lincoln, founded Brasenose, and Fox founded Corpus Christi College, both at Oxford. All of which (says Vergil) stimulated Colet, 'another Paul', to lecture in London and to found (we would say 'refound') St Paul's School. Vergil goes on to list the early high masters and ends: 'Just as the youth of London coming from St Paul's is greatly refined, so do classical studies (*perfecta literatura*) flourish in the whole of England.'[2] The curricu-

[1] *A Fifteenth-Century School-Book*, ed. William Nelson, Oxford 1956.
[2] *Anglica Historia*, pp. 145–7 collation.

lum was not transformed by magic: Colet's school was old-fashioned in its texts; but then Vittorino used Donatus and Villedieu and other old manuals,[1] and so did Guarino till he composed his own. The important achievement was that slowly but surely the schoolmaster emerged as a secular figure. He taught children for secular life, basing morality on Cicero as well as on the scriptures. He taught the magistrates and members of parliament so that they had libraries in their country homes and sent their children to be birched into the classics in their turn. He might even teach (as Roger Ascham did) a queen.[2] Education in England had been made lay by the mid-century—lay, Latin and virtually compulsory for the men who mattered, the gentlemen.[3]

If we look at France the picture is not dissimilar. The colleges at Paris, including the famous Collège de France itself, and the new schools in the provinces, like the Collège de Guyenne at Bordeaux, spread among succeeding generations the grammar and the morality hammered out in fifteenth-century Italy.[4] In the second half of the sixteenth century in France, as in England, we find the great men sending their children to school not to become clerks, but because they are gentlemen and may expect office and

[1] Manacorda, II, 240 ff.

[2] Despite the vast material available there is unfortunately no serious discussion of English grammar schools in the fifteenth and sixteenth centuries. The works by A. F. Leach and Foster Watson to which one perforce turns are jungles of undigested materials. The best account of the uses at which education *aimed* is still Woodward's volume on *Education during the Renaissance*, and the best account of what it actually was T. W. Baldwin's *Shakespere's Small Latine and Lesse Greeke*, 2 vols., Urbana 1944.

[3] J. H. Hexter, 'The Education of the Aristocracy in the Renaissance', *Journ. Mod. Hist.* XXII (1950), 1–20.

[4] I do not know of any worth-while history of French schools in the sixteenth century. W. H. Woodward's chapters on the subject in *Education during the Renaissance*, pp. 127–66, are worth reading.

employment, and because land and litigation and literacy go together. Hawking and games are now joined by Latin and Greek as the necessary preparation for life. The hatred for Latin thus engendered in many a boy was forgotten in later life when the tags and tatters of a classical education appealed to the adult man of business and the sententiousness of old age.

In these ways, and with a richness which I have been unable adequately to illustrate, the courtly North accepted the Italian Renaissance in its final courtly phase. It accepted the education in Latin grammar, the realism tempered with the heroic of High Renaissance art, the defence of the here-below as against the hereafter. There are, of course, all manner of cross-currents. A Reformation had happened, and something we call (I think it a misnomer) a Counter-Reformation. Broadly speaking the North became mainly Protestant and the South became[1] Roman Catholic. These religious differences may seem to obscure a little the fundamental cultural unity of late sixteenth-century Europe: but we should remember that Melanchthon, Calvin and Ignatius Loyola all prescribed in their schools the educational works of the Erasmus they all disliked and that the community of scholars over Europe as a whole was never stronger than it was between 1550 and 1700. Equally we may feel that diversity, not unity, set in with the rise of the vernaculars, to be reflected in all those 'battles of the books'—French *versus* Italian, ancients *versus* moderns and so on. I think this is not so. It was revived classical Latin which made the vernaculars flourish: the poets and dramatists and essayists, the theologians and the scientists of the

[1] *Became*—not (as we usually say) 'remained': but that is another matter.

late-sixteenth and seventeenth centuries were nearly all laymen, and they had all been to grammar schools. What might have caused a division was the ultimate triumph of humanist Latin itself: so great were its attractions that it is not, I consider, altogether impossible that it might have become a kind of mandarin language of the intellectuals.[1] This would have been disastrous. But the humanist schoolmaster taught men who turned their thoughts into French and English and German. With all their variations due to national temperament and background, the works of Rabelais and Montaigne, Shakespeare and Molière, Cervantes and Racine and Milton all belong to a common stock of Latin-nourished styles. They have a common ancestry, and we can trace it back to the moment when a passion for the humanities flourished in Florence in the late fourteenth and early fifteenth centuries.

When (one may fairly ask in conclusion) did this uniformity—which applies by the seventeenth century also in painting, architecture and music—when did this uniformity break down? When did a new uniformity begin to take its place? It is no more possible to say this with exactitude than it is to say precisely when the Renaissance begins. My own feeling, as I have tried to explain in chapter II, is that change is in the air at the start of the eighteenth century, during that *Crise de la conscience européenne* which has been so brilliantly described by Paul Hazard. At that point we begin slowly to move into a world where industry gains at the expense of agriculture,

[1] Cf. P. Villey, *Les Sources italiennes de la 'Deffense'*, Paris 1908, p. viii: 'une sorte de mandarinisme international'.

where the autocracy of the prince begins to be questioned, where national sentiment asserts itself as the focus of political passion, where the physical sciences, which (*pace* the historians of science) have played a minor role in the intellectual machinery of earlier ages, begin their steady upward rise as models of thought, as ultimate explanations. All of this takes time and does not bear fruit in different spheres at the same moment. Rousseau is already looking forward to a world of passion and sentiment while Burke is still looking back nostalgically to the ordered days of the past. Mozart and Beethoven stand—the Dante and Petrarch of music—the one a great summation of what has gone, the other with a programme for the future. In 1802 Constable painted 'Dedham Vale': we have moved from 'the Virgilian landscape' to the 'Wordsworthian'.[1]

From now on the writer and the painter try increasingly to catch a mood: in the Renaissance they told a story. Nature is now the great mistress, not the moral philosophy of antiquity expressed in Christian terms. As the nineteenth century moves on we finally leave Renaissance values behind. No humanist educator (and that is what all humanists were) would have felt comfortable in the age of the common man.

[1] '...just as the last chapter might have been called Virgilian landscape, so might this have been called Wordsworthian', Sir Kenneth Clark, *Landscape into Art*, London 1949, p. 78.

LIST OF REFERENCES

Studies marked with an asterisk are of particular importance

ALBERTI, L. B., *Tre libri della famiglia*, ed. F. C. Pellegrini and R. Spongano, Florence 1946.

*ALBERTINI, R. VON, *Das florentinische Staatsbewusstsein im Übergang von der Republik zum Prinzipat*, Berne 1955.

ALTAMURA, A., *L'umanesimo nel mezzogiorno d'Italia*, Florence 1941.

ARETINO, PIETRO, *Lettere*, sel. and ed. S. Ortolani, Turin, 1945.

BALDWIN, T. W., *Shakespere's Small Latine and Lesse Greeke*, 2 vols., Urbana 1944.

BALZANI, U., *Early Chronicles of Europe: Italy*, London 1883.

BANDELLO, M., *Tutte le opere*, ed. F. Flora, 2 vols., Milan 1934–5.

BARBARO, F., *De re uxoria*, see E. Garin, *Prosatori latini*.

*BARON, H., 'Cicero and the Roman Civic Spirit in the Middle Ages and the Early Renaissance', *Bulletin of the John Rylands Library*, XX (1938).

*——, *The Crisis of the Early Italian Renaissance*, 2 vols., Princeton 1955 (now revised in 1 vol., *ibid.* 1966).

——, 'Fifteenth-Century Civilization and the Renaissance', *New Cambridge Modern History*, I, Cambridge 1957.

*——, 'Franciscan Poverty and Civic Wealth in Humanistic Thought', *Speculum*, XIII (1938).

——, *Humanistic and Political Literature in Florence and Venice at the beginning of the Quattrocento*, Cambridge, Mass. 1955.

——, 'Secularization of Wisdom and Political Humanism in the Renaissance', *Journal of the History of Ideas*, XXI (1960).

BÉDIER, J., *Les Fabliaux*, 2nd ed., Paris 1895.

BELOCH, J., *Bevölkerungsgeschichte Italiens*, II, Berlin 1940.

BILLANOVICH, GIUSEPPE, *Petrarca letterato*, I, Rome 1947.

BILLANOVICH, GUIDO, '"Veterum vestigia vatum" nei carmi dei preumanisti padovani', *Italia medioevale e umanistica*, I (1958).

List of References

BIONDO, F., *Opera*, Basle 1531.

BISTICCI, VESPASIANO DA, *Lives* (The Vespasiano Memoirs), ed. W. G. and E. Waters, London 1926.

BOCCACCIO, G., *Decameron*, ed. V. Branca, 2 vols., Florence 1951–2.

BOSSUAT, R., *Manuel bibliographique de la littérature française du moyen âge*, Melun 1951.

*BOULTING, W., *History of the Italian Republics by Sismondi,...recast and supplemented*, London, n.d.

BRUNI, L., *Historiarum Florentini populi libri xii*, RR.II.SS. XIX, pt. 3, ed. E. Santini (1914–26).

——, *Dialogi ad Petrum Paulum Histrum* and *Laudatio florentinae urbis*, see E. Garin, *Prosatori latini*.

——, *Vita di Dante*, trans. P. H. Wicksteed, *The Early Lives of Dante*, London 1904.

*BURCKHARDT, J., *Civilization of the Renaissance in Italy*, trans. S. G. C. Middlemore, London 1929.

BUTTERFIELD, H., *The Whig Interpretation of History*, London 1931.

BUTTI, A., *I fattori della repubblica ambrosiana*, Vercelli 1891.

CAGGESE, R., *Firenze dalla decadenza di Roma al risorgimento d'Italia*, 3 vols., Florence 1912–21.

——, *Roberto d'Angiò*, 2 vols., Florence 1921–30.

CAMPANA, A., 'The origin of the word "humanist"', *Journal of the Warburg and Courtauld Institutes*, IX (1946).

CANTIMORI, D., 'Rhetoric and Politics in Italian Humanism', *Journal of the Warburg and Courtauld Institutes*, I (1937–8).

——, *Eretici italiani del cinquecento*, Florence 1939.

——, *Studi di storia*, Florence 1959.

CAROTTI, N., 'Un politico umanista del quattrocento: F. Barbaro', *Rivista storica italiana*, ser. 5, ii (1937).

*CHABOD, F., *Machiavelli and the Renaissance*, London 1958.

——, *Per la storia religiosa dello stato di Milano*, Bologna 1938.

——, 'Y a-t-il un état de la Renaissance?', *Actes du colloque sur la Renaissance*, Paris 1958.

CHASTEL, A., 'La légende médicéenne', *Revue d'histoire moderne et contemporaine*, VI (1959).

*CIPOLLA, CARLO, *Storia delle signorie italiane dal 1313 al 1530*, Milan 1881.

CLARK, K., *Landscape into Art*, London 1949.

COGNASSO, F., *see* Treccani degli Alfieri, *Storia di Milano*.

COHN, N., *The Pursuit of the Millennium*, London 1957.

COLOMBO, A., 'Della vera natura ed importanza dell'Aurea Repubblica Ambrosiana', *Raccolta di scritti storici in onore del prof. G. Romano*, Pavia 1907.

COMMYNES, P. DE, *Mémoires*, ed. J. Calmette and G. Durville, 3 vols., Paris 1924–5.

CROCE, B., *Storia della storiografia italiana nel secolo decimonono*, 2 vols., Bari 1947.

——, *Storia del regno di Napoli*, Bari 1925.

——, 'Recenti controversie intorno all'unità della storia d'Italia', *Proceedings of the British Academy*, XXII (1936).

DANTE, *Le opere*, ed. M. Barbi and others, Florence 1921.

DAUNOU, P. C. F., *Essai historique sur la puissance temporelle des papes*, 4th ed., 2 vols., Paris 1818.

DAVIES, KATHARINE, *Late Fifteenth Century French Historiography: R. Gaguin and Paulus Aemilius* (Edinburgh Ph.D. Thesis, 1954).

DE CAPRARIIS, V., *F. Guicciardini: dalla politica alla storia*, Bari 1950.

DECEMBRIO, P. C., *Opuscula historica*, RR.II.SS. XX, ed. A. Butti, F. Fossati and G. Petraglione (1925–58).

DE MATTEI, R., *Il sentimento politico del Petrarca*, Florence 1944.

DE MESQUITA, D. M. BUENO, *Giangaleazzo Visconti*, Cambridge 1941.

——, 'L. Sforza and his vassals', *Italian Renaissance Studies*, q.v.

DENNISTOUN, J., *Lives of the Dukes of Urbino*, ed. E. Hutton, 3 vols., London 1909.

DEVOTO, G., 'Per la storia delle regioni d'Italia', *Rivista storica italiana*, LXXII (1960).

DIONISOTTI, C., 'Geografia e storia della letteratura italiana', *Italian Studies*, VI (1951).

D'IRSAY, S., *Histoire des universités*, 2 vols., Paris 1933–5.

DOUTREPONT, G., *La littérature française à la cour des ducs de Bourgogne*, Paris 1909.

DU FRESNOY, LANGLET, *A New Method of Studying History…*, trans. R. Rawlinson, 2 vols., London 1728.

List of References

DURAND, DANA B., '"Il primato dell'Italia" in the field of Science', *Journal of the History of Ideas*, IV (1943).

EINSTEIN, L., *The Italian Renaissance in England*, New York 1902.

ELYOT, SIR T., *The Boke named the Gouernour*, ed. H. H. S. Croft, 2 vols., London 1880.

*ERCOLE, F., *Dal Comune al principato*, Florence 1929.

EUBEL, C., *Hierarchia catholica medii aevi*, 2nd ed., II, Munster 1914.

*FERGUSON, W. K., *The Renaissance in Historical Thought*, Cambridge, Mass. 1948.

FIUMI, E., 'Fioritura e decadenza dell'economia fiorentina', pt. III, *Archivio storico italiano*, CXVII (1959).

FOURNIER, P., *Le royaume d'Arles*, Paris 1891.

FUETER, E., trans. E. Jeanmaire, *Histoire de l'historiographie moderne*, Paris 1914 (see above, p. 133 n. 1).

GAETA, F., *Lorenzo Valla, filologia e storia nell'umanesimo italiano*, Naples 1955.

GANSHOF, F. L., *Histoire des relations internationales*, I. *Le moyen âge*, Paris 1914.

GARIN, E., *L'educazione in Europa 1400–1600*, Bari 1957.

*——, *L'umanesimo italiano*, Bari 1952 (in English, New York 1966).

——, 'I cancellieri umanisti della repubblica fiorentina', *Rivista storica italiana*, LXXI (1959).

——, see Treccani degli Alfieri, *Storia di Milano*.

——, ed., *Prosatori latini del quattrocento* (*La letteratura italiana*, ed. R. Mattioli and others, vol. 13), Milan 1952.

——, ed., *L'educazione umanistica in Italia, testi scelti*, Bari 1949.

GIBELIN, F., *Les châteaux de la Loire*, Paris 1957.

GILMORE, M. P., *The World of Humanism*, New York 1952.

*GOMBRICH, E. H., *The Story of Art*, London 1956.

GOOCH, G. P., *History and Historians in the Nineteenth Century*, London 1913.

*GOTHEIN, E., *Die Culturentwicklung Süd-Italiens*, Breslau 1886.

GRAYSON, C., 'Lorenzo, Machiavelli and the Italian Language', in *Italian Renaissance Studies*, q.v.

GREGOROVIUS, F., *History of the City of Rome in the Middle Ages*, trans. Hamilton, 8 vols. in 13, London 1894–1902.

GUERRI, D., *La corrente popolare nel rinascimento*, Florence 1931.

GUICCIARDINI, F., *Dialogo e discorsi del reggimento di Firenze*, ed. R. Palmarocchi, Bari 1932.

GUIRAUD, J., *L'État pontifical après le grand schisme: étude de géographie politique*, Paris 1896.

GUTKIND, C. S., *Cosimo de' Medici*, Oxford 1938.

HAY, D., 'The *Decades* of Flavio Biondo', *Proceedings of the British Academy*, XLV (1959).

——, *Europe, the Emergence of an Idea*, Edinburgh 1957.

——, 'Italy and Barbarian Europe', in *Italian Renaissance Studies*, q.v.

——, *Polydore Vergil*, Oxford 1952.

HEXTER, J. H., 'The Education of the Aristocracy in the Renaissance', *Journal of Modern History*, XXII (1950).

HOFMANN, A. VON., *Das Land Italien und seine Geschichte*, Stuttgart and Berlin 1921.

HOLT, E. G., ed., *Literary Sources of Art History*, Princeton 1947.

HOWARD, C., *English Travellers of the Renaissance*, London 1914.

Italian Relation, ed. C. A. Sneyd (Camden Society), London 1847.

Italian Renaissance Studies, ed. E. F. Jacob, London 1960.

JACOB, E. F., *Essays in the Conciliar Epoch*, 2nd ed., Manchester 1953.

JONES, P., 'Medieval Agrarian Society – Italy', *Cambridge Economic History of Europe*, i (2nd ed.), Cambridge 1966, pp. 340–431.

KOENIGSBERGER, H. G., 'Decadence or Shift? change in the civilization of Italy and Europe in the sixteenth and seventeenth centuries', *Transactions of the Royal Historical Society*, ser. 5, X (1960).

*KRISTELLER, P. O., *The Classics and Renaissance Thought*, Cambridge, Mass. 1955.

——, 'Petrarch's Averroists', *Bibliothèque d'humanisme et renaissance*, XIV (1952).

——, 'Il Petrarca, l'umanesimo e la scolastica a Venezia', in *La civiltà veneziana del trecento*, Florence 1956.

*——, *Studies in Renaissance Thought and Letters*, Rome 1956.

LEMAIRE DE BELGES, J., *Illustrations de Gaule*, ed. A. J. Stécher, 2 vols., Louvain 1882–91.

LEWIS, C. S., *English Literature in the Sixteenth Century excluding Drama*, Oxford 1954.

List of References

LOPEZ, R. S., 'Still another Renaissance' *American Historical Review*, LVII (1951–2).

——, 'Hard Times and Investment in Culture', in *The Renaissance, a Symposium*, New York 1952.

LUZZATTO, G., *Storia economica d'Italia*, I, *L'antichità e il medio evo*, Rome 1949.

MACHIAVELLI, N., *Discourses*, trans. and ed. L. J. Walker, 2 vols., London 1950.

——, *Il Principe*, ed. L. A. Burd, Oxford 1891.

MANACORDA, G., *Storia della scuola in Italia*, I. *Il medio evo*, 2 vols., Milan, n.d. [1914].

MANCINI, D., *Usurpation of Richard III*, ed. C. A. J. Armstrong, Oxford 1936.

MARZI, D., *La cancelleria della repubblica fiorentina*, Rocca S. Casciano 1910.

MASAI, F., *Pléthon et le platonisme de Mistra*, Paris 1956.

MAS-LATRIE, H., *Trésor de chronologie*, Paris 1889.

MASUCCIO SALERNITANO, *Il Novellino*, ed. A. Mauro, Naples 1940.

*MATTINGLY, G., *Renaissance Diplomacy*, London 1955.

Milano, Storia di, see Treccani degli Alfieri.

MOLLAT, G., *Les papes d'Avignon*, 9th ed., Paris 1949.

Monumenta Germaniae Historica: Leges, IV (2), Hanover 1909–11.

*MURATORI, L. A., *Annali d'Italia*, 12 vols., Milan 1744–9.

MUSSATO, A., *Ecerinide*, ed. L. Padrin, Bologna 1900.

MUSSO, G. G., 'La cultura genovese fra il quattro e il cinquecento', in *Miscellanea di storia ligure*, I (1958).

NARDI, B., 'Letteratura e cultura veneziana del quattrocento', in *La civiltà veneziana del quattrocento*, Florence 1957.

NELSON, W. (ed.), *A Fifteenth-Century School-Book*, Oxford 1956.

NISSEN, H., *Italische Landeskunde*, 2 vols., Berlin 1883–1902.

NOLHAC, P. DE, *Pétrarque et l'humanisme*, 2nd ed., 2 vols., Paris 1907.

ORIGO, I., 'The Domestic Enemy: the eastern slaves in Tuscany in the fourteenth and fifteenth centuries', *Speculum*, XXX (1955).

ORSI, P., *Signorie e Principati*, Milan 1900.

PALLUCCHINI, R., 'L'arte veneziana del quattrocento', in *La civiltà veneziana del quattrocento*, Florence 1957.

PALMIERI, M., *Della vita civile*, ed. F. Battaglia, Bologna 1944.

PANOFSKY, E., *Early Netherlandish Painting*, 2 vols., Cambridge, Mass. 1953.

——, *Meaning in the Visual Arts*, New York 1955.

PARKS, G. B., *The English Traveler in Italy*, I. *The Middle Ages (to 1525)*, Rome 1954.

PARTNER, P., *Papal State under Martin V*, London 1958.

PASCHINI, P., *Roma nel rinascimento* (Storia di Roma, XXII), Bologna 1940.

*PASTOR, L., *History of the Popes*, trans. F. I. Antrobus and others; vols. I–XII, London 1891–1912.

PERTILE, A., *Storia del diritto italiano*, vol. V, Turin 1892.

PETRARCH, F., *Epistolae familiares*, ed. V. Rossi and V. Bosco (edizione nazionale, vols. X–XIII), Florence 1933–42.

——, *Lettere...volgarizzate*, by G. Fracassetti, 5 vols., Florence 1863–7.

——, *Opera omnia*, 4 vols., Basle 1581.

——, *Secret*, trans. W. H. Draper, London 1911.

——, *De sui ipsius et multorum ignorantia*, ed. L. M. Capelli, Paris 1906; trans. by H. Nachod in E. Cassirer and others, *The Renaissance Philosophy of Man*, Chicago 1948.

PICCOLOMINI, AENEAS SYLVIUS, *Der Briefwechsel*, ed. R. Wolkan (Fontes Rerum Austriacarum, vols. LXI, LXII, LXVII, LXVIII), Vienna 1909–18.

——, *Commentaries of Pius II*, ed. and trans. F. A. Gragg and L. C. Gabel (Smith College Studies in History, vols. XXII, XXV, XXX, XXXV, XLIII), Northampton, Mass. 1937–57.

*PIERI, P., *Il Rinascimento e la crisi militare italiana*, Turin 1952.

PLATINA, B., *Liber de vita Christi ac omnium pontificum*, RR.II.SS. III, pt. I, ed. G. Gaida (1913–32).

RASHDALL, H., *Universities of Europe in the Middle Ages*, ed. F. M. Powicke and A. B. Emden, 3 vols., Oxford 1936.

RENAUDET, A. and others, *La fin du moyen âge*, 2 vols., Paris 1931.

——, *Les débuts de l'âge moderne*, Paris 1929.

*RENOUARD, Y., *Les hommes d'affaires italiens au moyen âge*, Paris 1949.

List of References

RICCI, P. G., 'Una consolatoria inedita del Marsuppini', _Rinascita_, III (1940).

RICE, E. F., JR., _The Renaissance Idea of Wisdom_, Cambridge, Mass. 1958.

Roma, Topografia e urbanistica di, by F. Castagnoli and others (Storia di Roma, XXII), Bologna 1958.

ROMANO, R., 'À propos du commerce du blé dans la méditerranée des XIVe et XVe siècles', in _Éventail de l'histoire vivante_ [à L. Febvre], 2 vols., Paris 1953.

ROSSI, MARIO M., 'Note sulla modernità del rinascimento', _Nuova rivista storica_, XXXIV (1950).

★ROSSI, V., _Il Quattrocento_, Milan 1938.

RUBINSTEIN, N., 'Beginnings of Political Thought at Florence', _Journal of the Warburg and Courtauld Institutes_, V (1942).

★——, 'Florence and the Despots in the Fourteeenth Century', _Transactions of the Royal Historical Society_, 5th series, II (1952).

——, 'Political Ideas in Sienese Art', _Journal of the Warburg and Courtauld Institutes_, XXI (1958).

RUSSELL, J. C., _British Medieval Population_, Albuquerque 1948.

★SABBADINI, R., _Il metodo degli umanisti_, Florence [1922].

——, _Giovanni da Ravenna_, Como 1924.

★——, _Le scoperte dei codici latini e greci ne' secoli XIV e XV_, 2 vols., Florence 1905, 1914.

★——, _Storia del Ciceronianismo_, Turin 1886.

SACCHETTI, F., _Il trecento novelle_, ed. V. Pernicone, Florence 1946.

SALUTATI, C., _Epistolario_, ed. F. Novati, 4 vols. in 5 (Fonti per la Storia d'Italia), Rome 1891–1911.

——, _Invectiva in Antonium Luschum vicentinum_, see E. Garin, _Prosatori latini_.

SALVEMINI, G., _Studi storici_, Florence 1901.

SANDYS, J. E., _A History of Classical Scholarship_, II, Cambridge 1908.

★SAPEGNO, N., _Il Trecento_, Milan 1934.

SAPORI, A., 'Medio evo e rinascimento, spunti per una diversa periodizzazione', _Archivio storico italiano_, CXV (1957).

SAXL, F., _Lectures_, 2 vols., London 1957.

SCHLOSSER, J., _Die Kunstliteratur_, Vienna 1924.

SETTON, K. M., 'The Byzantine Background to the Italian Renaissance', *Proceedings of the American Philosophical Society*, C (1956).

*SIMEONI, L., *Le signorie*, 2 vols., Milan 1950.

SIMONE, F., *La coscienza della Rinascita negli umanisti francesi*, Rome 1949.

*——, 'Sur quelques rapports entre humanisme italien et humanisme français', in *Pensée humaniste et tradition chrétienne*, Paris 1950.

SIMONETTA, G., *Rerum gestarum F. Sfortiae commentarii*, RR.II.SS. XXI, ed. G. Soranzo (1932–4).

*SISMONDI, S. DE, *Histoire des républiques italiennes au moyen âge*, 16 vols., Paris 1809–18; *and see* W. Boulting.

SORANZO, G., 'Collegati, raccomandati, aderenti negli stati italiani dei secoli XIV e XV, *Archivio storico italiano*, XCIX (1941).

*SYMONDS, J. A., *The Renaissance in Italy*, 7 vols., London 1875–86.

TENENTI, A., *Il senso della morte e l'amore della vita nel rinascimento*, Turin 1957.

THEINER, A., *Codex diplomaticus dominii temporalis S. Sedis*, 3 vols., Rome 1861–2.

TILLEY, A., *The Literature of the French Renaissance*, 2 vols., Cambridge 1904.

TOFFANIN, G., *Che cosa fu l'umanesimo*, Florence 1929.

*——, *Il cinquecento*, 3rd ed., Milan 1945.

——, *Storia dell'umanesimo dal XIII al XV secolo*, 3rd ed., Bologna 1947.

TRAPP, J. B., 'The Owl's Ivy and the Poet's Bays', *Journal of the Warburg and Courtauld Institutes*, XXI (1958).

*TRECCANI DEGLI ALFIERI, Fondazione, *Storia di Milano*, vols. V (1310–92), VI (1392–1450), VII (1450–1500), Milan 1955–6.

ULLMAN, B. L., 'Some Aspects of the Origin of Italian Humanism', *Philological Quarterly*, XX (1941).

——, *The Origin and Development of Humanistic Script*, Rome 1960.

VALENTINI, R. and ZUCHETTI, G. (eds.), *Codice topografico della città di Roma* (Fonti per la Storia d'Italia), III, IV, Rome 1946–53.

VALERI, N., *L'italia nell'età dei principati del 1343 al 1516*, Verona 1950.

List of References

VALLA, L., *Scritti filosofici e religiosi*, trans. and ed. G. Radetti, Florence, 1953.

VASARI, G., *Le vite de' più eccellenti architetti, pittori et scultori italiani da Cimabue insino a tempi nostri*, in *Opere*, ed. G. Milanesi, 9 vols., Florence 1878–85.

VERGIL, P., *Anglica Historia*, ed. D. Hay (Camden Series), London 1950.

VILLANI, G., in *Croniche di Giovanni, Matteo e Filippo Villani*, 2 vols., Trieste 1857–8.

VILLEY, P., *Les sources italiennes de la 'Deffense'*, Paris 1908.

——, *Les sources d'idées au XVIe siècle*, Paris 1912.

VINAY, G., *L'umanesimo subalpino nel secolo XV: studi e ricerche*, Turin 1935.

VOIGT, G., *Eneas Sylvius Piccolomini als Papst Pius II*, 3 vols., Berlin 1856–63.

*——, *Die Wiederbelebung des classischen Alterthums*, 2 vols., 3rd ed., Berlin 1893 (see above, p. 68 n. for other eds. and trans.).

VOLPE, C., *Medio evo italiano*, 2nd ed., Florence 1928.

*WEISE, G., 'Il duplice concetto di Rinascimento', *Rivista storica italiana*, LXVIII (1956).

——, *L'Italia e il mondo gotico*, Florence 1956.

*WEISS, R., *The Dawn of Humanism in Italy*, London 1947.

——, 'The Greek Culture of South Italy in the Later Middle Ages', *Proceedings of the British Academy*, XXXVII (1951).

*——, *Humanism in England during the Fifteenth Century*, 2nd ed., Oxford 1957.

——, *Un umanista veneziano, Papa Paolo II*, Venice 1957.

——, 'J. van Eyck and the Italians', *Italian Studies*, XI (1956), XII (1957).

——, 'Learning and Education in Western Europe from 1470 to 1520', in *New Cambridge Modern History*, Cambridge 1957.

——, *Il primo secolo dell'umanesimo*, Rome 1949.

WHITE, J., 'Developments in Renaissance Perspective', *Journal of the Warburg and Courtauld Institutes*, XII (1949), XIV (1951).

WHITE, LYNN, JR., 'Tibet, India and Malaya as Sources of Western Medieval Technology', *American Historical Review*, LXV (1959–60).

*WHITFIELD, J. H., *Petrarch and the Renascence*, Oxford 1943.

WILKINS, E. H., *The Making of the 'Canzoniere' and other Petrarchan Studies*, Rome 1957.

WITTKOWER, R., *Architectural Principles in an Age of Humanism*, London 1949.

WÖLFFLIN, H., *Classic Art*, trans. P. and L. Murray, London 1952.

*WOODWARD, W. H., *Vittorino da Feltre and other Humanist Educators*, Cambridge 1897.

*——, *Studies in Education during the Age of the Renaissance*, Cambridge 1906.

ZABUGHIN, V., *Giulio Pomponio Leto*, 2 vols. in 3, Rome–Grottaferrata 1902, 1912.

——, *Storia del rinascimento cristiano in Italia*, Milan 1924.

ZEEVELD, W. G., *Foundations of Tudor Policy*, Cambridge, Mass. 1948.

IX Congrès international des sciences historiques, *Rapports*, Paris 1950.

X Congresso internazionale di scienze storiche [Rome], *Relazioni*, VI, Florence 1955.

INDEX

of subjects and the more important places and persons

Index

Index

Index